ETCHING FOR THE HEART

Kalu Onwuka

Granada Publishers

Los Angeles, California

Etching for the Heart

Copyright ©2014 by Kalu Onwuka

Published in Los Angeles, California by Granada Publishers. Granada Publishers is wholly owned by Granada Publishing Company, Los Angeles, California.

Granada Publishing titles may be purchased in bulk for educational, fundraising or sales promotional use. For more information please e-mail **sales@granadapublishing.com**

All rights reserved. No part of this publication may be reproduced, stored in a retrieval system or transmitted in any form or by any means-electronic, mechanical, digital, photocopy, recording or any other-except for brief quotations in printed reviews, without the written permission of the copyright owner.

Library of Congress Cataloging-in-Publications Data

Etching for the Heart/ Kalu Onwuka

LCCN: 2014918588

ISBN: 978-0-9900203-6-3

ISBN: 0990020363

Printed in the United States

DEDICATION

I will like to dedicate *Etching for the Heart,* which is the part of *Ruminations on the Golden Strand* series, to all those who share the gifts of light and love everywhere in the world either in formal or informal settings. Yours is not an easy task for Truth is very hard to tell and often falls on deaf ears in a world where the sweet and easy has become the norm. The world may or may not acclaim you but Heaven's promise is never to forget or forsake such as you that labor to keep the gate against the onslaught of darkness.

ACKNOWLEDGMENTS

As always, I will first like to acknowledge Christ Jesus as the Lord of my life. He is my muse and I write through his light. Also, I will like to acknowledge that it is not possible to see through an undertaking such as *Ruminations on the Golden Strand* series without the loyal support of family, friends and well-wishers. You have all been there from the beginning on through to the publication process. I will like to acknowledge all your assistance for you continue to give me cause to hope for better from mankind. It is such goodness that you show that will help transform the world from what is today to the better that it can be tomorrow.

CONTENTS

Dedication   iii

Acknowledgments   iv

Introduction   vii

Chapter 1   Abounding in Full Light   1

Chapter 2   Pare the Flesh for Life   11

Chapter 3   Transformed in Light   19

Chapter 4   Star that Never Dims   27

Chapter 5   Passageway of Light   37

Chapter 6   Up to the Summit   49

Chapter 7   Love that asks for Little   59

Chapter 8   Entrusted with the Key   69

Chapter 9   New Gifts and Skills   79

Chapter 10   A Standard of Reference   89

Chapter 11   Heaven records All   99

CONTENTS

Chapter 12	From Water into Life	109
Chapter 13	Assurance of the Faithful	119
Chapter 14	Great Vision and Strong Faith	127
Chapter 15	Under Divine Sunshine	139
Chapter16	Marks of the New Life	147
Chapter 17	Peace for the Certain	157
Chapter 18	Light in a Dark Sea	171
Chapter 19	The Sons Wait to Sing	181
Chapter 20	In the Wilderness	191
Chapter 21	From the Sacrifice of One	203
Chapter 22	Script for a New Life	213

INTRODUCTION

Etching for the Heart is the third volume in the well-received *Ruminations on the Golden Strand* series. The series encapsulate experiences gleaned during faith walk and in the aftermath of spiritual transformation following the light after Christ Jesus. There are also numerous insights and observations drawn from real life that help to frame the truth shared within these pages in a way that readers will find very interesting.

No one can re-connect with God unless he has been purified in spirit through the light of Christ. Spiritual purification is like a baptism of fire whereby the seeker is proven to be worthy of Christ or not. There is attendant pain endured in this baptism as well as associated costs that many are not willing to pay. However, for the willing it is an irreversible process that brands them as worthy to be counted among God's chosen. The latter are able to walk in the fullness of divine light and by extension become the light for others to follow. To be chosen in this light is a call that only God makes on mankind's life as he only knows who can endure the branding in fire. For one, the branding takes place in life's wilderness as the chosen will be rejected by the worldly. It is branding that makes one to be in the world but to be no longer of it.

However, there is a pre-requisite to the baptism of fire.

Introduction

The heart has to be washed by the word of Truth before it can be ready to be branded as belonging to God. Mankind has to accept the word of God as absolute Truth and commit to its obedience before he can commune with the Divine. Acceptance and commitment to Truth leads the seeker to step back from the worldly so as to step forward towards God. Truth serves as a filtration membrane in the heart to help turn the polluted waters of the worldly into crystal living water that sustains new life in the light of Christ. It is only when the filtration process is in place and operational that the baptism in fire comes about so that the seeker can be baptized in spirit and reborn in Christ.

The believer that has been baptized in the fire of the spirit through Christ will awaken to a new reality. He will find that he has become a different creature from what he used to be and must resist the tendency to return to where and what he left behind. He will be disappointed if he does so for he will not find satisfaction in it. It is old wine that will fall short of the new that he has already tasted. He will be better off to realize that the glory of the new that is now available to him through Christ is far greater than that of the old which must be left behind. It takes some time for the baptized in spirit to understand the scope and nature of what he has become in God through Christ. But the faithful believer soon does as he embarks on a lifelong odyssey of discovery to accomplish many things in the spirit and power of the living God.

Humanity has just about entered the season where much

Introduction

is being accomplished in the spirit of the Divine. This is the noon time of the harvest of men's souls by God. It is the harbinger of things to come and a pre-cursor to the renaissance of Eden. Only those hearts washed and souls purified by Truth have a place assured for them in this final season. It is at this time that the seedlings for the new age are being gathered. The looming new age is for those with the full anointing of Christ able to commune with God in spirit. The new age will be a congregation of the purified in spirit and noble of soul made 'perfect' through Christ. For those remade in that light, life does become a celebration of the victory of the spirit over the flesh.

At the same time, the season of the full blossom of the fruits of the tree of knowledge of good and evil has beset mankind. Many are gouging on it and harbor the feeling of empowerment. But it is only a delusion of empowerment that has unleashed a flood bound to leave many spiritually dead in its wake to cast them adrift in a sea of the unneeded and poisonous. And so, the collective consciousness borne of the information deluge of this age carries mankind down a vortex of destruction as if being flushed down a toilet by the hand of divine judgment.

The journey to be branded in the heart and bonded as one with Christ is a long and wearying one. But it is the only means to be re-connected with God. It leads the weary traveler through the inevitable valley of the shadow of death which can be quite unsettling. It usually ends in a

Introduction

place of blessed quietness far removed from the noisy and pestering so that the still small voice of God can be clearly heard. The voice heard is that of the Holy Ghost which avails information to the faithful in real time from heavenly places. It is such information that guides and enables the faithful to re-create his surrounding in accordance with Divine will. He that is privy to the Holy Ghost will bear testimonies from heavenly places.

Every bearer of testimonies from heavenly to earthly places is a watchman that dwells on the spiritual housetop. He reports about those things gleaned from a heavenly perspective so that those without such knowledge can know through him. The faithful who dwells on the spiritual housetop has yielded his life to the sovereign will and service of God. He is able to have foreknowledge of events that loom on mankind's horizon. He that has yielded his life in this wise, will be endued with veiled knowledge. He will be entrusted with the hidden so that he may be of best service to God and humanity.

Hidden truth or the sacred is availed from heavenly places to include insightful knowledge and wisdom needed to address certain situations encountered in life. He that is privy to the veiled will have the words to pierce through the veil of darkness to reach the hardened heart. He that can do that will induce the willful and hardened heart to yield for goodness to abound and show forth from him.

The bearers of such knowledge that can change mankind

Introduction

within are called to use that gift to reshape those 'flattened' by life's troubles into vessels worthy of use by God through Christ. The sinful always resist the way of life that the light of Christ affords for it is a mirror of indictment in which mankind's evil and wicked ways are exposed. It may be inconvenient and discomforting to be confronted by one's ugliness but it helps mankind to know true self. He that does not know his true self will never be free in spirit. He will be a poisoned fountain whose words will lack power and a damaged pillar who cannot withstand evil. Such that is poisoned and damaged cannot afford the fulfilling and enduring availed through Christ.

Profession may be from the mouth but true confession is always from the heart. Mankind's redemption in true light becomes possible when the confession of his heart is in harmony with the profession out of his mouth. When such becomes the case, a sense of release and freedom of spirit will frame daily living. A sense of serenity and peace within inevitably follows suit for then the confessor will be divinely embraced as an embodiment of Truth.

This book is not a substitute for the Holy Bible but only serves to amplify the eternal truths that are found there. As the reader goes through this volume, I hope that the contents will help to enlighten minds and reshape hearts into vessels ready to serve the Divine will in truth and love so that humanity can become collectively better.

Kalu Onwuka

Charity needs not parade to be noticed

Seeks neither attention nor recognition

Yet its light can never ever be obscured

For the universe always searches it out

Chapter 1

ABOUNDING IN FULL LIGHT

All true spiritual paths indeed converge in Christ as the light of the world and vestibule into the heavenly Father's abode. The faithful know to receive and welcome the teachings of Christ into the heart for thereby some duly become transformed in the likeness of divine image. The latter are the new vessels that are able to receive the new wine that God offers humanity through Christ. They are sanctified in Truth and give voice to that which the spirit of God speaks into their hearts. Many have been positioned as nodes of his kingdom of light to lend their voices in good faith and serve humanity in love through Christ.

God has positioned his sons all over the world in every country, culture and tongue. It is a world wide web governed by the Holy Spirit that pulses with divine ethos and Christine pathos. These sons of light are privy to that which the heavenly Father has purposed for humanity. It is knowledge communicated to them in spirit. As such, they live under the impulse of the spirit of the heavenly Father and act in faithful accord with his divine will. In a non-contrived yet certain way, they have come to model Heaven on earth for their thoughts and footsteps are earthly impressions of godliness used to highlight Christ.

Baptism in the word of Truth or good knowledge of the teachings of Christ is commendable as that which man can accomplish through his mind and flesh as he serves God. Although very admirable, such will always fall short in man's bid to meet up with Christ. Beyond baptism in the word of Truth is baptism in spirit or the realm of Christ where all is accomplished under the mercy of God. With baptism in spirit it is no longer man's mind and flesh but the Divine that acts through him to carry out earthly endeavors. It is for this reason that Christ Jesus declares on one hand that in serving God there is none born of woman that is greater than John the baptizer in water. On the other hand, he also declares that the least that has been 'born again' into the kingdom of God or baptized in divine spirit is greater than John. In order to be greater than John, the believer has to mature in spirit past what he can do on his own into what God can use him to do for divine glory. The believer has to be reborn in the spiritual likeness of Christ Jesus so as to be worthy of use for the glorious and everlasting.

Humanity has just about entered the season where everything needs to be accomplished in the spirit of God and no longer by that of the world. For all intents and purposes, the season of the spiritual harvest of the soul of humanity has just about dawned as a precursor to the renaissance of paradise. Only those hearts washed in Truth and purified in light through Christ are being gathered in this season as seedlings for the looming paradise. This new age of Heaven on earth is for those bestowed with the anointing of Christ that God can commune with in spirit. It is a place for the congregation of the noble in spirit made perfect in Christ. Like old wine that has turned sour, the age of the flesh has just about run its full course. The faithless whose flesh has not yet been subjugated has no place in the new Heaven on earth for life therein is the grand celebration of the victory of the spirit.

The professed believer in whom the flesh is predominant over his spirit is not rooted in faith. He is not yet fully established in grace and remains far from standing before God under mercy. The spirit which engenders selfishness, contention and destructive anger will rule him. He will lack the ability to speak and act in grace for he has not made ample room for Christ. He will be covetous and not easily satisfied for he is empty on the inside. On the other hand, the spirit of the faithful who has been fully established in grace will have his flesh under subjugation to become selfless through Christ. He will be given to stand before God in mercy as due and in accordance with divine will. To abound in grace to stand under mercy is Christ realized by the faithful and that by which God's kingdom is increased.

The faithful believer that abounds in grace will always have the right words for all situations to exhort and teach in love through Christ. He will be easily satisfied in soul for he has been filled up with the essence of the everlasting. Such never craves the materials but cares for the spiritual. He is given to pursue peace and seek justice for all with no fear of the ungodly for he knows that God's eye is on him always to protect and meet his needs. He knows that he is equipped for noble service and required as a good steward to give good account of all that God has entrusted to him.

Sadly many presume to be wise in their own eyes and have concluded falsely that grace is without accountability. On account of such false presumptions they are denied access to the true wealth of God received only under his mercy. In becoming misguidedly wise in own eyes, such have become blinded and view grace as a means for material bounty. But he that trusts that divine Providence remains assured will be faithful to partake honorably of grace and be duly established to stand before God in mercy. It is to such who prove worthy of grace that God entrusts with the true riches of his kingdom. It is to them that true knowledge and divine wisdom is availed to overcome the bedeviling issues of life. God never fails to commune with such in spirit to inform their mind and to make them spouts to offer up the living water of wisdom.

The wise in the world have become spiritually blind to the

true riches of God. Through greed and unbridled lust, they have come to lack the right hand of righteousness with which to receive the holy and sacred upon which the kingdom of God is founded. Having loved the world too much, they have lost their souls therein. For such the left hand, which is the hand with which to deal with the world, may have been fortified but the right hand has withered from lack of use. It is the right hand which symbolizes and governs all of man's righteous activities on earth. Where the right hand has withered, man's handiworks will not be pleasing to God but an ostentatious display aimed at drawing praise from men. And so, all blinded by greed often attempt to cover self with self-glorious undertakings that count little for charity but not much in the divine scheme. The love of the world darkens the heart and prevents love for Christ. He who loves the world will never have Christ within and therefore will lack true charity.

Unless the believer has been established through grace on to mercy he cannot truly live charitably for Christ. Charity is the essence of Christ and embodies acts of selflessness performed out of pureness of heart as burnt sacrifices for the benefit of others. Many have concluded falsely that charity is about material undertakings. It is much more than that for charity is really about sacrificing effacingly for the benefit of others in love. It involves time, effort, and lastly materials. It takes unfeigned love and that hope which never gives up. The charitable in spirit denies self the wants of life so that the recipient can receive the needful things that he cannot afford otherwise. There may be both a real and an opportunity cost associated with every act of charity. True charity pleases the heavenly Father very much, counts very much in the divine scheme and is rewarded wherever such governs mankind's actions.

Charity is an expression of the essence of Christ which is to live in service of others. Charity aims to bring mankind into the enlightening and revelatory light of God. Where true charity has been rendered, the recipient will inevitably receive a glimpse of the Divine. Charity is that which leads the compassionate of heart to give selflessly and in love in the spirit of Christ. Such is neither an indication of abundance nor a statement of being well off but every endeavor carried out in the spirit of universal brotherhood. Every true act of charity should be a burnt sacrifice and should evoke the sweet fragrance of the offering well received in its wake.

Every one that lives effacingly in selfless sacrifice so that others can glimpse the better light of the divine way will always be guided in true light. He that is so guided will be given to see himself as the captain of a boat in a world filled with the blind and helpless. He will assume it to be a sacred duty to help as many as he can navigate through life's stormy seas to safety. To fulfill such a sacred duty demands a lot of sacrifices along the way in a selfless spirit that places others first before self. The selfless rejects all that is contentious but often rather chooses to make do with little as the case may be. In choosing to do so, he in effect chooses to dwell on the corner of the 'housetop' so that his eyes can remain fixed on God. He chooses to do so in order to be that dutiful watchman that looks out for the welfare and safety of all charged to him. From his vantage point on the spiritual housetop, he is able to have knowledge of looming and impending events. All who are still bound by the things of the world cannot come up to the 'housetop' for it is only for those willing to forego all so that the will of God may be fully known to them. It is for those who have embraced charitable living and retreated in spirit into the heavenly Father's cocoon of love.

The faithful whose eyes are truly fixed on God will become aware of certain ordinances and statutes. Those two are vitally needed for welcome into the kingdom of God. Ordinances have to be observed so that the 'passageway' into the kingdom of God may be ascertained. An ordinance works more or less like a spiritual blinder needed to keep the glare of worldliness away so that the faithful believer can maintain focus on the prize ahead and carry on in good faith. After an ordinance has been known and kept in good faith, a statute is next revealed for the faithful in the way to observe.

Observance of the ordinance helps to point the faithful in

the direction of the 'passageway'. Observance of the statute affords the faithful the spiritual fortitude to navigate through the 'passageway' into the kingdom of God. Observance of the ordinances and statutes can be accomplished through Christ and make for spiritual passage into the kingdom of light. Where the ordinance is not known, the way remains hidden and where the statute is not observed, the spiritual will to overcome obstacles in the way will be lacking. Charitable and selfless living in the service of others yields the knowledge of the ordinances and statutes but living in the spirit of Christ enables their fulfillment. It is in this wise that Christ or christening in divine light is the 'passageway' or the tunnel of light that leads into the kingdom of God.

Heaven on earth is a re-enacting of charitable living by all and for all in the light of Christ. True charity is humble, seeks not its' own, does not count costs or return evil in kind. The new Heaven on earth will be governed by the golden rule of oneness and togetherness of spirit. This land of hope is a place of charity where each one's wish is his brother's command in love. It is for the purified of soul who can soar in spirit to where the magnificence and glory of God reflects on all. It is the place of everlasting new songs, the font of poems and of good works.

Chapter Highlights

- ✓ The thoughts of the sons are impressions and their footsteps stamps that define the way of Christ.
- ✓ The way of the 'Nazarite' is admirable but it pales in light with that of the 'Nazarene' through Christ.
- ✓ The new age is for hearts washed by Truth and souls purified in the fire of the spirit of Christ.
- ✓ The faithful believer abounds in grace and so has the right words to ameliorate all situations.
- ✓ It is in the bowel of mercy that the true wealth and riches of God availed through Christ are found.
- ✓ The handiwork not committed to God is weariness for the soul for it will not endure or shine in light.
- ✓ True charity has a real and an associated cost but it brings mankind to the place close to God's heart.
- ✓ True charity aims to bring mankind into the enlightening and revelatory light of God.
- ✓ The spiritual housetop is for those willing to forego all so as to remain privy to the will of God always.
- ✓ The washing of the soul by Truth helps mankind to perceive the way into the kingdom of God.
- ✓ The land of charity is where none is denied for each one's wish is his brother's command.
- ✓ The land of charity is a place of new songs, font of poems as well as all good works.

All's realized in a future safe from the past

With appointments in Providence to keep

And rendezvous with the Divine to make

In the light of Truth and warmth of love

Chapter 2

PARE THE FLESH FOR LIFE

The watchman on the spiritual housetop is a bearer of testimonies from heavenly to earthly places. He is one that shares knowledge witnessed from his place of vantage above with the earth-bound in love. The faithful whose spirit dwells on the housetop has yielded his life to the sovereign will and service of God. He is able to have foreknowledge of events that loom on the horizon and thereby keep many from being blindsided.

All who are endued with knowledge in this wise will have the information necessary to navigate through expected as well as unexpected challenges. The call to the spiritual housetop is for the watchman who has devoted himself to the welfare of the flock. The flock may be little or large but size matters not in the kingdom way. Little is much when God is in it. The faithful watchman is often made aware of the veiled and is privy to transformational changes about to take place within humanity. He is the herald of the new thing that God is about to do so that the attentive believer may be prepared for it. The new thing that God always does is always the replacement of the shallow and lacking with the deeper and fuller.

The watchman in essence travels ahead to the place of the new thing which is always a place of regeneration or the remaking of the future in an image that is a reflection of the spirit within man. As the spirit within yields to the divine sovereign will, the future travelled to will reflect the heavenly abode. Conversely as the spirit within man disobeys the divine will, the future travelled to will reflect the antithesis of Heaven. The spirit that yields to the Divine moves forward in time to a brighter future but the spirit that disobeys moves backwards in time to mankind's darker past. The spirit of Christ moves the faithful forward into a more humane future but the spirit of the enemy moves the faithless backwards in time to a beastly past. The spirit of Christ affords the faithful the knowledge to bring new things out of the old. To the contrary, the prince of the darkness of the world avails the faithless the knowledge to take new things back to the old.

The watchman is able to see where humanity is blindly headed towards and is used by God to offer a course correction. Mankind finds itself in its present dilemma and spiritual morass because he has disobeyed God for too long. Yet the heavenly Father continues to hold out hope by availing mankind a way out through the light of Christ.

The same urgent call that was answered and the same duty that was assumed by the prophets of old has gone all over the world today beseeching mankind to embrace God's way in order for humanity realize better. The prophets of old were always vilified in their times but always borne out to be right in the end. Sadly it is no different but remains same today as God pleads with and implores mankind to embrace true light through Christ. Christ is a cleansing spirit that washes away the mud cakes of the misguided past so that a pristine dawn can be ushered in for humanity. When that is done, mankind can begin to feast with love and live in true enlightenment to the heavenly Father's delight.

The word of Truth does not tell mankind what he likes to but what he needs to hear. It is Truth that addresses areas of weakness to strip away any illusions that mankind harbors about his spiritual worthiness before God. The scriptures have been written down so that man can search out the Truth about his Creator and his place in creation. The Holy Bible lays out the beginning and the end for the earth as well as the creatures that live in it. It contains the record of man's origins, reason for his creation and the two ways which face him while on earth. It shows where either road ends and highlights the dual composites of the earthly as well as the spiritual that constitute man.

In effect, the scriptures bridge the gap from the beginning

to the present so that man may be better informed about who he is, why he is here and where he is going. There is a constant effort within the scriptures to make a distinction between the two overarching ways of life on earth and a constant reminder of the end result of either way. Life in the hereafter for both man and the earth is fully addressed as well as the nature of the next age of the 'new earth'. Put simply, the words of scripture make up the guiding manual for life on earth so that mankind can heed to be awakened to reflect the Divine. The inner man of the spirit is the true self and it has to be alive for man to find peace and fulfillment on earth. It is Truth laid out in the Holy Scriptures that leads mankind to reconciliation and reconnection with his Creator so that he can exchange restlessness within with an assured peace.

There is a central covenant between God the Creator and man the creature. God, who can never lie, has made certain promises to man in good faith. The heavenly Father expects man to live his life a certain way in accordance with God's laws. God gives freely to mankind from his divine largesse but it is not without accountability. It requires obedience to God's laws in order for man to have the result of his earthly endeavors fulfilling. Disobedience to the laws voids God's promises to man and disconnects him from the flow of divine power. He who lives his life on earth in faithful obedience to God's laws will remain in good covenant, grow to spiritual maturity and reconnect with God duly. The faithful man that has reconnected with God has exchanged the short-lived of the earthly for the everlasting of the heavenly. Such has been guided to become purified in true light so that he can exchange corruptible flesh for the spirit of eternal life.

God is fully aware of man's spiritual blindness and makes room for it by allowing him enough time to travel on both paths of life. He has also left a spark of his goodness in everyman to prompt him to choose his path wisely. This enables mankind to experience as well as be able to evaluate the pitfalls and benefits of either choice that he makes. There is the choice of living God's way and trusting him to fulfill his covenant promises. Then there is the alternative choice of living in the world's way which ends in spiritual death and nothingness in the hereafter. God is long suffering and willing to patiently wait until the season of grace runs out for each man. The season of grace is critical for it is when God is very near and may be found easily by mankind through Christ. The things concerning Christ do come to an end and each man must therefore take advantage of the window of grace when it is open.

The window of grace is never closed when there is a child of God earmarked for salvation left to be saved. God is never in a rush nor is the store of grace exhaustible. However the window of grace closes after it has run its due course and there is none worthy to be saved. After such a course, both the contrite and the hopelessly lost soul would have had occasion to repent. The contrite soul will expectedly begin to seek after God and grow in faith. But the hopeless soul will remain unrepentant and lost in the world. It is for the latter that the window of grace closes. Meanwhile the erstwhile sinner who returns to God's way in sincere repentance and good faith will enter into a season where more grace is poured into him even as it runs out for the unrepentant. The erstwhile sinner who becomes truly repentant will always abound in grace.

There is really no end to grace for as it closes for some on one level it opens fully for others on a higher one as mercy. He who uses his given talents well will receive more but he that does not will be dispossessed of the little that he has. Grace never ends but at some point of divine accountability, it closes for the unworthy partaker who is after his own gain. But the believer who has been a worthy partaker and sharer of grace will grow to be established in faith. He will be established from grace to more grace until the door is opened for him to stand before God in mercy. God's long suffering nature must not be taken for apathy or his patience misjudged for impotence. The heavenly Father exhausts all means to save mankind so that in the end the soul lost forever has no one to blame but self.

Chapter Highlights

- ✓ The watchman on the spiritual housetop bears testimony from the heavenly to earthly places.
- ✓ The faithful are endued with knowledge needed to overcome expected and unexpected challenges.
- ✓ The faithful that yield to God's sovereign will realize a future on earth that reflects the heavenly.
- ✓ The spirit within is only able to digest the meat of Truth when the misguided past is left behind.
- ✓ Truth speaks to address areas of weaknesses and spare man from the delusion of self-righteousness.
- ✓ Only by reconnection with God can man satisfy his spiritual hunger and find fulfillment in life.
- ✓ There is a spark of goodness in man to help him choose between the way of life and that of death.
- ✓ The worthy before God are used to make profound impact on those ear-marked for salvation.
- ✓ He who seeks God in repentance receives more grace but the window closes for the unrepentant.
- ✓ The worthy in grace grow to be established in faith until they can duly stand before God in mercy.
- ✓ The faithful that has been adopted into the divine household has come into faith rest and Providence.
- ✓ A sad and regrettable tale is that the hopelessly lost soul has no one to blame but self.

The golden apples of wisdom are received

By faithful hearts in good and timely order

As pearls that decorate their attentive ears

In a dawn of the lovely under divine mercy

Chapter 3

TRANSFORMED IN LIGHT

The faithful believer that stands before God under mercy has scaled up in spirit to the mount of transfiguration. The latter is the mountaintop where the pure dew of heaven descends and all things therein reflect the glory of God. He that is able to stand there has been faithful to live by the laws of God written in his heart. The mount is a place for the righteous that are pure of heart and have goodwill for all humanity. Most men know what God requires and what his laws demand from them but choose not to obey. He that knows and lives by the laws written in his heart will be counted among the worthy duly given in spirit to mount up to the place of transfiguration.

The mount of transfiguration is a place where all that come desire to dwell and not depart from. It is the place where the faithful believer becomes transformed in light and is given to eat the fig from the tree of life. He who eats from that tree can see the pictures veiled in the scriptures. He who eats from the fig tree will be afforded a place in the kingdom of light. He will have insight into all that is needful both for the present and future. He that is transformed in this light will live by and for Truth. Therefore all things that are untruthful will feel exposed in his presence. It is for this reason that such is one who is under unceasing attack by the prince of the darkness of this world. But nothing can harm him who lives by Truth for he will be under a dome of divine protection. He may suffer temporary loss in the world but he will gain back even more in due time for he is one for whom Providence invariably saves the best for last.

He who has gone up the mount of transfiguration has received the passport into the kingdom of God through Christ. He has become transformed in spirit to become one who may be surrounded by troubles but not touched by it. He will come to realize the peace which passes all understanding so that while the storms of life rage around him, he will remain unperturbed for he has found rest in Christ. One is able to scale the mount of transfiguration through faith in God, love for Christ as well as fellow man. It takes selfless sacrifice to afford the footholds necessary to ascend the mountain and the light of Christ to avail the vision necessary to 'see' the footholds along the way.

There is no other way to scale the mountain of faith or obtain the passport into the kingdom of God. It is not obtained by financial means, heritage, intellect or other worldly considerations. It is obtained by living in the spirit of new life in Christ and in hope for God's commendation. The faithful welcomed into the kingdom of light is able to receive apples of wisdom from the divine applecart and to turn such into pictures of silver that can be seen with earthly eyes. The apples of wisdom are hidden truths revealed only to the faithful. Such are prescient knowledge and inside information divinely availed so that the faithful can be well informed always. The apples of wisdom constitute the means by which God showers his love and sheds his glory on the faithful.

The hidden truths are revealed in love to pierce the darkened veil and bring light into faithless hearts. Such is given to discomfort and rid mankind of the notion that sin can be concealed. Sin can be hidden from men's eyes but not from God's all-seeing eye or all-knowing mind. When God uses the faithful to speak forth certain truths, the intention is not to humiliate or mock the sinner but rather to shine loving light in the hope that correction for better can result. The light of Truth is shone in the hope that the sinner can change his ways while there is still a chance of escape for him. It is shone so that the uncertain can reset his heart to God and perhaps find redemption at last. It is shone in good hope and redeeming love in an attempt to save his soul for God loves man that much.

Freedom from the bondage of darkness that still blinds

his soul far exceeds the seeming discomfort that the sinful may experience in the light of Truth. The faithful believer that has been freed from the bondage of darkness is bestowed with the spirit of power and a sound mind. He will be emboldened to speak Truth from the lowliest to the highest as the case may be for he will not be slack in holding up the standards of God for all to see. The free in spirit and transformed in light is often used to give voice to the divine urge from heavenly places. As such, his voice is given to ring out loudly and clearly as a herald of redeeming hope to declare to anyone who will receive Truth to come in before the door of the ark is shut.

The faithful called to service in this light must be strong of faith and firm in spirit to withstand the assaults of the enemy. He must be the representation of the good soldier who fights for light against darkness in noble duty to serve God and humanity. The good soldier embodies the triumphant spirit that will not give up hope even when there seems to be no longer reason to do so. He embodies the spirit of love that will not let go until the last vestige of the strangleholds of darkness on humanity has been loosed. He embodies the spirit of goodness triumphant that defines the redeemed through Christ and the best that humanity can yet be.

The spirit of goodness triumphant is appointed for the peaks of mankind's spiritual ugliness. The time of spiritual ugliness is when things look good on the outside but rotten on the inside. It is a period of unparalleled hypocrisy when there is a façade of spiritual purity without but unbridled moral decadence within. It is a period of massive deception when humanity appears to be going one way but is actually heading in the opposite direction. It is a time of the grand masquerade when the prince of darkness is at his most devious posing as the messenger of light. It is a season when God's heart aches and breaks on account of mankind's sinful ways.

The ugly period is the time of the proliferation of temples of worship and the swelling of religious congregations. On the surface it would seem that there is a great spiritual revival going on but in Truth the collective soul of humanity has gone after the material things of the world. It is Baal worship reprised to leave the collective soul of humanity marooned on the parched desert of wantonness. The ugly period is a time of great anguish in Heaven as the corruption of the human soul stinks up to there. A change is always inevitable when evil becomes prevalent and pervasive. And so, needed change is now well underway and forthcoming to usher in God's searching light where nothing ugly can hide.

The ugly period is when the spiritually blind lead the people instead of the enlightened of God. It is a time when men prefer might over right and the wrong appear to be strong. The ugly period is when the professed followers of Christ will not recognize the true man of God in their midst. However those who seek after true light in good faith with love for God in their hearts will know wherever Christ has come to full life. A sad commentary about earthly living is that many who are close to light are sometimes blinded and not know to benefit from it. But those who are far from same do recognize and embrace it to duly receive sight thereby. The ugly period concludes with the withdrawal of the hand of God's blessing on mankind which results in severe hardships for many. But for some, it is a time when the hand of God is near to shield his true servants while exposing the true nature of the false confessors who exploit his name for gain.

The ugly period is a time when man can ill afford to go by sight because he will be easily deceived. Rather it is a time for him to go in the spirit of God for that will be his only faithful guide. He who has been bestowed with the spirit triumphant has been given the wherewithal to thrive in ugly times. He will shine brightly then for it is in the dark times that true light is known. He will blossom as a garden perfumed with many fruitful trees for it is then that God makes the handiworks of the faithful to come to full light.

Chapter Highlights

- ✓ The faithful grows from grace to scale the mount of transfiguration and stand before God under mercy.
- ✓ The faithful in Christ who stand before God under mercy have insight into all the needful in life.
- ✓ The faithful transformed in the light of Christ may be surrounded by troubles but not touched by it.
- ✓ The transformed receive wisdom to be turned into pictures of silver that can be seen with man's eyes.
- ✓ Wisdom calls the faithful to justify his freedom by helping others to become free too.
- ✓ The faithful is bestowed with the spirit of power and sound mind so as to speak Truth to all as fit.
- ✓ The transformed in light embodies a nobility of spirit that leads mankind to offer his best to God.
- ✓ The ugly season is when the prince of darkness is at his most devious posing as a messenger of light.
- ✓ The ugly period is a time of great anguish when mankind's corruption stinks up to Heaven.
- ✓ The season of spiritual ugliness is when the blind lead the people instead of the worthy before God.
- ✓ The faithful with the spirit triumphant has been availed the wherewithal to thrive in the ugly times.
- ✓ A sad commentary about mankind is that those who are close to light are often dismissive of it.

Drought or deprivation is often ordained

To play a transforming role in a man's life

It is through the times when he is in lack

That he comes to know what's important

Chapter 4

STAR THAT NEVER DIMS

There is a burden of responsibility that comes with sharing the message of Christ in good faith so that the spiritually blind can see. Every true bearer of light understands that he is a custodian who not only has to keep the flame of Truth alive but must share it so that others can see in true light. He that lends voice to share Truth in the spirit of Christ will be divinely entrusted with much in due time to include the hidden and secret things of Heaven. He that has been entrusted with such by the heavenly Father is called to share in love with others as due and as urged. He is never to deny any that comes in humility and sincerity.

The bearer of divine light is only a messenger who comes so that the people may have due knowledge and cease from stumbling around in darkness. He is often times saddled with a lingering feeling that perhaps he has not done enough in discharging this calling. He feels that he may have failed in some measure in the fulfillment of his duty to God and man. He often wonders if he spoke too long, too short, too loud or too soft in the discharge of this sacred duty. At other times, he wonders if he was too impatient or too accommodating in his approach. Because he knows that the word of God is true, he tends to blame himself if he fails to win over that targeted soul for God. But he need not worry or burden himself with such thoughts for the battle is not his to win but God's. The messenger is only there to serve God's commanding will. He is called to lend his body as a vessel to be used by the spirit of God to do work and need not worry about immediate results. Whenever and wherever the Spirit of God is involved nothing is ever lost regardless of how unfruitful things may appear to be.

The fact is that every time that the faithful messenger responds to the impetus within and shares the word of Truth in good faith, he has done well. He has discharged his duty diligently. He is called to cast the seed and leave it to the Spirit of God that led him to speak in the first place to open up the heart of the hearer to receive the Truth shared. The sower of the word is only a servant who obeys the will of his divine Master. It takes the Spirit of God both to will and act through the sower as well as the hearer of the word to make the encounter fruitful. The sower must take heart in the knowledge that the word of God does not return void but accomplishes every purpose for which it is uttered. It is living water that will either produce good fruit in the receptive or tares in the resisting heart.

Often times the bearer of light feels a burden of guilt. He often wonders why he is made to hear, speak, know, understand and see but not the next fellow for he does not see himself as more deserving or worthier. He is prone to stretches of contemplative silence during which he dwells on these thoughts as well as words of Truth that have been laid on his heart. More often than not, he will not open his mouth to speak unless when necessary for his actions rather than words speak of his devotion to God, love of Christ and abiding hope for humanity. The bearer of light is bestowed with a divine mind and therefore sees the world in a different light. He sees it from a divine perspective as one that looks in from a higher spiritual perch. He is often the lone voice that speaks to shed light in truth, correct as needed, uphold with grace, encourage in love as well as sound the necessary alarm in a world which considers him to be a strange one.

Sadly many are spiritually blind in the world and often accuse the messenger of crying danger where there is none. To the blind, mankind should do better with his time on earth than listen to God out there that cannot be seen. But the faithful who can see know that the world is a snake's pit that requires mankind to be spiritually awake or risk being infected with its venom as the unwary and blind find out soon enough. Though often dismissed the bearer of light must persevere in his calling while making room for ignorance of the blind. He knows that the blind are shrouded in dimness of soul and muddle along to the delight of the masters of the darkness of this world. The bearer of light labors under the burden of love mingled with sorrow for he knows what sad consequences await blind and unwary mankind in this world and hereafter. His life's work though hardly appreciated on earth causes great joy in Heaven. The bearer of light may not be accounted for much on earth but he will never lack reason to be thankful for Heaven will always bless him in love.

Thankfulness to God for everything encountered in life is essential for all who hunger for righteousness before him. He who has been established through grace to stand righteousness before God knows to be thankful in life always. Such fully understands that thankfulness for blessings received makes for a humble spirit and keeps God near. Thankfulness to God for gifts received in Christ is the lubricant that maintains the flow of grace. It refreshes parched souls and revives flagging spirits. It sustains the spirit of the bearer of light in times of discouragement when his words seem to fall on deaf ears and weariness leads him to wonder if he has labored in vain. For all who labor for the spread of light, there are unguarded moments when doubt does creep in. Thankfulness to God for prayers answered keeps such moments of doubt at bay and the divine connection intact.

Thankfulness to God for his goodness and tender mercies opens the ear of the heart. When the ear of the heart is opened, the tongue is often loosened to praise God. The voice that is tuned to praise God will have the window of Heaven always open for him. The whole of God's creation joins in when there is genuine praise being rendered to the Creator. The thankful heart will always see improvements take place and healing break out in all areas of his life. It takes an 'opened' ear to hear the inaudible voice of Truth. Thankfulness to God helps to reassure the heart and keep the noise of the world away so that the spirit within can acquiesce for the inaudible to be clearly heard. Thankfulness for hope of eternal life in divine company keeps the ear of the heart well-tuned so that the believer is able to hear as creation sings God's praise to join along. The melodious harmony of all things in the universe comes through clearly to the thankful heart so that he knows that he is not alone but part of a whole. The unthankful heart will never experience fullness in life for he will be like one that has lost a precious coin. Thankfulness on the other hand, avails mankind the coin needed to pay the toll on the road to fullness in life.

On the way to fullness in life, every faithful believer will pass through a season of deprivation in his life. Deprivation or the cessation of rains is divinely ordained in the life of every man so that he may be able to sort out his life. It is through the season of deprivation that mankind is able to determine what is important in life and what is not. Often times the unimportant things take up room in life to inhibit and obstruct mankind from finding God. When the unimportant things are identified and let go, man finds to his surprise that he is not far from the path of righteousness. He may not be on that path yet but he will find through the light of Truth that he is not far from it. The weeds that choke life's garden have to be removed so that the fruitful can bask in the sunshine of divine love.

When the rains cease, the ugly weeds of life shrivel so that the lovely and enduring can have the needed room to be established. The lovely and enduring things come from the heavenly Father who gives good gifts to the faithful. It takes three years for roots of the good to be established through grace. It also takes the same period for roots of the ugly weeds of life to wither. The cessation of the rains may bring deprivation with it but it is of more harmful effect to the unfaithful than the faithful. The faithful believer does not suffer as much for his needs are handy and easily met. He is one that has contentment of soul in whatever state he finds himself. He has learned through Christ that contentment with godliness is very gainful for mankind and therefore suffers through deprivation with grace in the assured knowledge that Providence will cater to all his needs always.

Deprivation eradicates or chokes the ugly things in the life of the believer so that the lovely can have room to be established and blossom. The cessation of the rains is part of the baptism of fire through which the faithful must pass through to meet up with Christ. He may be brindled on the outside but his inner core will remain unscathed. He will remain the same within the spirit in any circumstance that he finds himself in life. The faithful who is brindled without but unscathed within has become purified so that he can move on to produce good and enduring works of glory as a good tree pruned to produce abundantly.

He that is purified through the baptism of fire can ascend in spirit to the mountain top where the rain clouds are found and is called to be a rain maker. The purified of heart is given to bring back the rains to the valley where it is sorely needed to refresh thirsty souls that dwell there. He is the water bearer who holds the power of restoration for the people. He can bring back life to the dead and dying. His footsteps lead without fail to the place where provision can be found for the needy. When his footsteps falter in weariness, the heavenly Father picks him up for he is much treasured as a 'precious pearl' that God keeps in the palm of his hand. The purified of heart is a priceless vessel prepared by the heavenly Father for such glorious service that he reserves for the sons. The purified of heart is a temple of the living God whose soul has been immersed in the everlasting dew of immortality.

The faithful that is immersed in the everlasting dew of immortality is truly blessed for goodness and mercy will attend him on earth. Others choose the building of monuments to honor God and by extension themselves. They receive the accolades of men and earthly rewards for their undertakings. But the bearer of divine light is himself a monument to God. As a joint heir of the new Heaven on earth with the other sons of light, he has chosen to forego material rewards but to seek after the blessings of the heavenly Father. He may be blamed for the troubles of the land but it is the transgressions of the people that trouble the land. He may be despised because he speaks about things unseen and unknown by the blind masses. He may be despised because he can venture forth where others cannot go. He may be despised for countless other reasons, yet his love to serve God remains unwavering for Truth is too good and important to be neglected.

The bearer of divine light never takes rejection to heart. He forgives for many know not what they do and carries on in faithful duty as love urges him. What he knows and has, he holds in trust for the people as divine gifts received for the blessing of all. He cannot cease in the mission of Christ for he lives in the kingdom where the will of the Father urges all to act in love. The fragrance of eternity and the glory of the Father rest upon the bearer of divine light whose heart is a star that never dims but shines so that the past, present and future can join in glory.

Chapter Highlights

- ✓ He that speaks Truth has proven to be faithful in little and will be entrusted with much by God.
- ✓ The bearer of divine light is sent so that the people can have due knowledge and cease from stumbles.
- ✓ The messenger has done well every time that he responds to the urge and shares Truth faithfully.
- ✓ It is mankind's action rather than words that speak to his devotion and love for God.
- ✓ The bearer of divine light is not accounted for much by the world but Heaven rejoices over him.
- ✓ Thankfulness to God in all things keeps moments of doubt at bay and the divine connection intact.
- ✓ The voice that is tuned to praise God in Truth will have the window of Heaven open for him always.
- ✓ When weeds that choke life's garden are removed the fruitful therein bask in divine sunshine.
- ✓ The cessation of the rains may bring deprivation but the needs of the faithful will always be met.
- ✓ Deprivation is often necessary for it chokes the ugly so that the lovely can have needed room to thrive.
- ✓ The bearer of light is a rain maker who brings down the mountain dew so that life can be revitalized.
- ✓ The bearer of light always carries on in faithful duty for the light in him is a star that never dims.

The faithful dwell in the eternal stream

As utility vehicles always ready to serve

Such are duly fitted and well configured

To weather trouble and trials unscathed

Chapter 5

PASSAGEWAY OF LIGHT

The believer that rides the passageway of light is a spiritual messenger who ascends in spirit from the earthly to heavenly places to receive gifts. He descends again to the earthly realm to offer these gifts to mankind in love in accordance with divine will. A life dedicated to this cycle of receiving from God above and sharing with mankind below is ordained to be used to alert the receptive to things that require due attention. Such is information that helps to guide mankind in the direction that God is leading so that the receptive is not blindsided by events.

The rider in light is a mediator between heavenly and earthly places tuned to hear the still small voice that speaks to man's heart. The voice heard within is the voice of Truth which originates from the throne of God. The fact of the matter is that God is Truth. The believer that speaks and lives by Truth will be sanctified in same and given to ride the passageway of light that leads to the divine heart. He that has been sanctified in Truth is tuned to hear the voice of the Holy Ghost which enables mankind to receive due knowledge and information from the divine throne above. The gift of the Holy Ghost affords the receptive knowledge of the future so that he can be duly informed and truly guided in divine light.

He that rides the passageway of light is well prepared as a vehicle of the Divine to weather myriad trials and overcome challenging circumstances in life. He will pass through the stormy wind to prove him, earthquake to validate him and test of fire to reveal his core content. He is able to pass through such tests and overcome his trials without compromising his integrity because he is securely anchored on Christ. The stormy wind is the harbinger of drastic change. It manifests as a 'stream' that floods humanity's consciousness and leaves many 'dead' and deluded in its wake. It leaves a human wasteland of road-kill of people alive in the flesh but dead in spirit. It has already been manifested in the onslaught of the internet. Never in the history of mankind has he been inundated with so much information. The information age as the internet will bear out is a platter that will seem to serve goodness in the beginning but devolve to serve the bad and the ugly mostly in the end.

As the information age devolves, the season of the full blossom of the fruits of the tree of the knowledge of good and evil will beset mankind. He will deliriously gouge on it and harbor the feeling that he has become empowered. But it is only a delusion of empowerment for it is a flood that will cast mankind adrift in a sea of unneeded information and leave many spiritually dead in its wake. No one can resist the fury of the flood and none can direct its path once the raging starts. Everything and everyone in its path will get swept along. And so, the collective consciousness borne of the information deluge of this age is poised to carry man down a vortex of destruction as if being flushed down a toilet by the unseen hand of divine judgment. Mankind's helplessness in this unfolding cosmic affair notwithstanding, he has chosen to continue in his delusion of being empowered rather than yield in spirit for God direct his earthly affairs.

An earthquake follows in the wake of the stormy wind to bring down the things that have been weakened by the flood but still standing. The quake is already being felt all over the world. It quakes to bring down the needless things. It quakes to separate the things that have deep roots and are anchored on the bedrock of Christ from the things that are not. It quakes to affirm those who are at peace within and sway in rhythmic harmony with divine accord. All who are on God's side will be left standing but all else will be brought down by the quake. Long standing institutions previously considered too mighty to fail will fall. Many of the proven engines of the industrial age will falter and others will come to a halt. Bastions of economic power and political arrangements that have withstood the test of time will crumble. Society's pillars of morality will turn out to be wanting and prove to be ethically unworthy. Many such institutions that are highly regarded will not withstand the earthquake as all things that stand with the 'feet of clay' will be brought down. All things that have utilized size, reach and bluster to control the people will be brought down. The quake is much like a pebble used by the divine to bring down the unwieldy and unsustainable in the same wise as David brought down Goliath.

A fire soon follows after the quake to determine the souls that will continue in the new age of the earth. These are those faithful believers who have passed judgment to be 'sanctified' in Truth. The currency of the new Heaven on earth will be Truth. In taking short cuts, bending corners and compromising Truth in order to gather earthly possessions, many have failed to lay up treasure in heavenly places. Such will hardly pass the test of fire and fail to meet the standard for the new age to come. But he that has embraced Truth to much discomfort and loss in this world will easily pass judgment for a place in the new.

Every rider of the passageway of light is given to pass through the flood of information age but not be deluded or overwhelmed by it because he has due knowledge. He has no interest in knowing all things for he has knowledge of the needful. He has knowledge of the pertinent and prescient due to the Holy Ghost who informs him. He that is availed the Holy Ghost will commune well with his surroundings and be tuned into that needed for the day. For that reason, he is not encumbered by much in life and so remains well focused on God. Pertinent and prescient knowledge allows mankind's footsteps to be guided in accordance with divine will so that he can remain standing through every quake. He does not become disoriented or lose focus because he is not overly encumbered in life. He is not overly burdened because he is laden within with seeds of the needful and fulfilling in life. He knows who he is in God through Christ and can walk the strait path for he knows where life is taking him.

The rider of the passageway of light is sanctified in Truth. He speaks and lives by Truth for it shields and protects him through the fire of judgment unscathed. He is not turned to stubble because Truth oozes the dew of the oil of the anointing of God. The anointing is a fire wall and retardant that protects the faithful as he passes through the fiery. He who has passed through the stormy wind, the earthquake and the fire becomes the rider of the passage way. He is one that the divine hand has lifted up into a realm of higher consciousness unlike the decrepit who are being flushed down the pit of oblivion.

The spirit of the world is evil that masquerades as Truth. The world has come into a season when the best of humanity have been extracted. Life on earth is but a divine distillery to purify and separate worthy souls from the debased. The catalyst for this purification process is the light of Christ. Life as mankind has known it in this age has just about run its course. The message of Christ has been availed to mankind everywhere. Many have embraced its light but others have rejected Christ to deny themselves the new life which he brings. It is for this reason that the mission of Christ is about concluded. The bridegroom has entered into his bride chamber and the door is about shut.

The best of humanity have been extracted and lifted up into a higher consciousness. The ones lifted up in this wise are the riders of the passageway of light who intermeddle between the heavenly and earthly. Such live on a higher plane of the new Heaven on earth in spiritual fellowship with other purified souls in God's kingdom of light where the pleasing, fulfilling and enduring can be experienced. The rest of mankind has been left behind to sink into a lower pit of consciousness as debased souls. Having souls that are debased, these are no better than beasts. For them, the world has become a place of the carnal and a carnival of the flesh where the debased are but soulless dogs feasting on other dogs. Put simply, humankind has just about been sorted into its best and worst with a new firmament in place to keep both apart by divine mandate. The new firmament will separate those who live by the flesh from those who live in the spirit of new life in Christ.

A new re-creation of the existing has just about been completed as God sorts out and re-arranges the earthly to reflect the heavenly order.

Space and time are always bound together in a way clearly understood. One can only be physically present at one place at a certain time while another may be at another place at the same time. And yet another may be at a different place at that same time. By extension, many can be at different places at a certain time. Even though such are scattered far and wide from each other, yet their spirits can dwell in same place by sharing common faith. The matured in spirit can travel beyond the confines of the flesh from wherever they may be physically located to the exalted realm where such congregate. The matured in spirit who can travel beyond the flesh in this light has bonded with Christ as one among the riders of the passageway of light whose meeting place is around the mercy seat of God. Such that can travel in spirit to the exalted realm have died in the old nature of the temporal and are reborn in the new light of the eternal. For them, a better new has come to life from the carcass of the old.

The faithful that are bonded with Christ have become sons of God in divine light. They can travel to the meeting place of the sons in spirit through the passage way of light and return again to the earthly plane to carry out the will of God as ordained above. This labor of commuting in spirit to the exalted realm and back will continue as long as the earth remains. It is this labor of love that stays the hand of divine justice and affords humanity hope until all the work ordained by God to be done on earth is completed. It is only then that the curtain will fall and the firmament of separation between the heavenly and earthly sealed up.

On the contrary, many people can be at the same place at the same time but their spirits may be in different places because they do not share common faith. The exalted realm is not appointed for those who profess same faith but for those matured in Christ who confess in truth and worship God sincerely. In other words, out of the many physically present in one place at the same time, only one person may be matured in spirit to bond with Christ. He may be in that place or in that world physically but not of it in spirit. The faithful that is not of the world is only a brief visitor until the time appointed for his return home. Time as man measures it ceases to exist for those that have become bonded with Christ. All who ride the passageway of light have become timeless. They are intrepid travelers in the spirit of universal love who sow seeds of goodness so that the divine way can abound.

Mortal man is under the earthly clock as well as the cosmic clock. The earthly clock is there to remind mankind that he has only limited time to search out the way and re-connect with his divine roots. He must do so within an allotted time while he is alive on earth before time runs out for him. He who finds the way in timely order has escaped both the ravages and constraints of earthly time for he is given to live in spirit in cosmic time. He will come to live under the cosmic clock which runs interminably even as the universe itself does. He has gone from being an earthling to become a universal being. But those who cannot find their divine roots in allotted time will remain hopelessly lost in darkness in an endless loop under the earthly veil. They will remain stuck on earth tied to its foreboding fate with no hope of escape. This is the sad fate of the spiritually blind and that to be avoided.

Although far from such because of its implications for everlasting life or death, one is tempted to look at it as a cosmic game of hide and seek in which man must seek and find his way back to the heavenly home before his allotted time on earth runs out. The fear of time running out on him is symbolized by man's euphoric elation at the last second shot made in a basketball game or the field goal kicked through as the time runs out in a football game. Man knows in his subconscious mind that humanity is under a quest to find the way home and that the earthly clock is running out. The last second shot made gives him hope. The field goal kicked through in the nick of time tells him not to despair. He who finds the way home to the heavenly Father in allotted time will live forever. He that has found the way has received the greatest gift.

He who has found the way home has escaped the trapping of space-and-time. Space and time emanate from the divine throne. Mankind is availed life to occupy space on earth on account of divine mercy. He is afforded time on earth by God so that he may use it for good works. In that light, mercy and goodness are translatable in space and time. Divine mercy abounds in those places or availed to the heart where time is used for goodness of humanity. He that has goodness and mercy as earthly attendants is given to receive the gift of eternity. In as much as space can never be separated from time neither is mercy ever separated from goodness.

Mercy and goodness are reflections in which the face of the Divine can be glimpsed by mankind in space-and-time. The faithful hear the still small voice of God in space-and-time and follow through by matter and energy in acts of mercy and goodness. It takes space-and-time divinely ordained through the light of Christ to order matter and energy in the heavenly way. And so wherever divine will is communicated and served in good faith, matter and energy will give cause to space-and-time to look heavenly. The riders of the passageway of light have learned to yield to divine will in all matters and are therefore able to order their earthly environments to reflect the heavenly.

Chapter Highlights

- ✓ The believer that speaks and lives by Truth will be divinely appointed to ride the passageway of light.
- ✓ The traveler in light is a vehicle who has been prepared by God to weather storms and trials.
- ✓ The spiritual earthquake serves to validate things that have deep roots and are anchored on bedrock.
- ✓ Many fail to lay up treasures in heavenly places by the compromise and dishonor of Truth.
- ✓ The rider of light is lifted into a divine realm while the spiritually blind stumble on in darkness.
- ✓ Truth is a distillery to separate the purified from debased souls with light of Christ as the catalyst.
- ✓ The faithful can be in different locations but dwell in same place in spirit by sharing common faith.
- ✓ Men that do not share common faith can be in same place but dwell in different places in spirit.
- ✓ Man that fails to find the way back to the home above in due earthly time will remain lost forever.
- ✓ Mankind must reconcile with God in due time so that he can reclaim his gift of immortality.
- ✓ Mercy and goodness are the vehicles by which the heartbeat of the Divine can be felt on earth.
- ✓ The essence of the Divine is revealed in things that God touches for such will always shine before all.

The endearing voices of goodness and mercy

Motivate the travelers in the eternal stream

Those who do certain things at certain times

To idealize matter and energy in space-time

Chapter 6

UP TO THE SUMMIT

The journey to meet up and become bonded as one with Christ is a long and wearying one. But it is the only means for mankind to find the way home to the heavenly Father. It inevitably leads the weary traveler to a place of blessed quietness that is unsettling initially. It is a place that takes getting used to in order to appreciate its full blessings. This spiritual state of being is far removed from the noisy and pestering so that the still small voice of God can be heard with clarity. The voice heard there speaks in love from the heavenly throne and is amplified when Truth is embraced. It is the voice of the Holy Ghost heard only by the truly faithful which pleads with all men to pay heed to God. He who is tuned to the Holy Ghost receives information in due time and good order from heavenly places to guide his footsteps in accordance with divine will.

The place of blessed quietness is the mountain ledge upon which the weary traveler rests in preparation for the final ascent to the summit of faith. It is a quiescent and tarrying state where the bread of life laden within the believer is converted into spiritual meat. Although the believer is weary, this is the time to re-dedicate to searching out God's Truth anew. It is necessary to re-dedicate to searching out the word anew for the harmony within all scriptures can be known in purer and greater light. There is no cloudiness of mind in this state where all things can be made plain and nothing is hidden anymore in its pure light. It is the place where the faithful must overcome his fear and learn to use his wings. He will not need his legs to climb up to the summit but his wings. Unbeknown to him, faith has turned his hands into wings. He has become one given to no longer strive in his own might and power but to achieve with divine assistance through prayer. He can only find that out as he lets go and lets God.

However it can be a time of fear and trepidation for the valley seems so far away. In order to make it to the summit, the seeker has to be at rest completely in Christ else he will not make it to the holy mount of God. It is like shifting gears when driving a vehicle. Before he can ease into the gear of Christ the believer must disengage from the gear of the worldly. The road that he has sought out is the high road of life on which contentment with godliness will prove to be far better than the material attractions of the world that he has left below. The seeker must be completely at peace within in the reality of his new being in Christ so that he can fully realize the godliness that comes with it. Total submission to Christ is the only way for the seeker to be able to harness the services available at this stage of the climb to overcome any obstacle ahead.

He that has made it to the summit of the holy mount has passed judgment in the fire of the spirit of Truth. The baptism of fire confers the anointing of the spirit of God on the faithful believer to infuse his words with an urgency that mankind cannot help but consider. He that has passed judgment in the fire of Truth is one whose heart has been lit to become an altar to God. Fire symbolizes the divine gift that keeps man 'comfortable' and chases away his fear of darkness in the wilderness of life. Baptism in the fire of the spirit of Truth is the means to burn away the unproductive things in life so that the new and better can have room to bloom. The faithful that has passed judgment in the baptism of fire can offer up burnt sacrifices that will be well received by God. All his acts of charity will be well received above for his heart has become an altar lit with the flame of love and dedicated to serving humanity in love.

He that has passed judgment in the baptism of fire has a divine calling to bring the light of the full moon to brighten the night time of human understanding. The night time is when there is a lack of sufficient knowledge and therefore a lot of stumbling around by mankind. Night time is also when ugly deeds are carried out under the cloak of darkness. He that is baptized in the spirit of Truth brings due knowledge that turns night into day. He brings needed light so that mankind will stop stumbling on account of fear, doubt and lack of true knowledge. He brings the full moon of divine accountability so that the ugly deeds of darkness will cease. He that brings light into darkness is one able to make the spiritually blind see.

There has never been a darker season and a more appropriate time in mankind's existence for those baptized in the spirit of Truth to bring the light of the full moon of accountability into the life of the people. He that has passed judgment in the fire of Truth serves God and humanity best in the spiritual night time. The latter is the inglorious season of excesses where men worship at the altar of wealth and a man's worth is measured by his material possessions. It is this misconception used by the spiritually blind to validate earthly existence and prove a man's worth that those who can 'see' must help to correct. It is a quite a sad and misconceived idea for mankind to believe that he who acquires the most materials has won life's race. Nothing can be further from the truth for material possessions do not equate to wholeness and counts for nothing at the end. Yet the mad quest for materials has pulled the collective soul of humanity downwards into self-destruction where the end justifies the means. The notion that the end justifies the means now drives mankind to do the shameful and sinful.

It is of no concern to mankind if the future generation is damned. Yet it is by this faulted reasoning that one must acquire as much of the world's bounty as he can that has led many to take God out of life's equation.

It takes special strength of character forged in the crucible of faith and trust in divine Providence for one to choose a life contrary to the order of the day. To go contrary to the world is no mean feat. Certainly the choice to trust God with one's earthly lot does cost in the short term. It has cost some everything and has put others at the risk of loss of life. But whatever the seeming obstacles, the believer who endures through hardship will discover at the end that he was never forsaken or really alone for God was there with him. The journey of faith exacts much from the believer but often the result is to make him an immortal soul connected with the Divine. He that is connected in this wise becomes an indefatigable rider on the passageway of light who lives for all ages. Such is the life lived as a burnt sacrifice well-received by God that brings hope back to the people when it is needed most.

The life lived as an embodiment of the sacrifice well-received by God requires absolute commitment. A definite choice between the love of the way of God and that of the world has to be made by the believer in order to realize it. It is not a life lived in uncertainty, partaking of the world or straddling the fence as it suits one's purposes. Straddling the fence, so to say, is the recipe for spiritual ugliness where mankind's dark intentions and misdeeds can be mischievously covered with feigned spirituality. It is a sham display whose cloak is a thin veneer that wears out soon enough to expose the despicable ugliness within.

Ugliness that hides within mankind's soul is borne of an unclean spirit that attempts to halt the spread of God's light. It is the serpent in its most enchanting and fatal form. It is the spirit of darkness that masquerades as the messenger of light. It induces uncertainty in the seeker so as to choke the flow of the power of God. Uncertainty of faith taints and makes the would-be vessel unclean before God. It is like a viral infection that makes the professed believer to veer off course and not fulfill his mission. Only by certainty of faith can the believer be baptized in the spirit of life through Christ so that he can afford the antidote to the venom of the unclean spirit.

The power of God works mightily where there is certainty of faith to effect transformative changes in many areas of life. It makes the best to come out of the worst of men. It makes the cowardly of heart to become brave. It confers wisdom on him considered to be foolish by the world. It changes the anger prone into a man of peace for it tames the beast in man. It turns the man of many weaknesses into the virtuous and valiant. The believer of many foibles who becomes certain in faith in the light of Christ will earn

God's trust to have his prayers readily answered for he has become a courier of life to where death stalks.

Hedging one's bet with God may be considered a smart move by many but it is really an act of foolishness. It shows a lack of faith in that it presumes that God is not able to deliver as he promises. The power of God does not show forth mightily when and where the professed believer hedges his bet for it does not flow fully in uncertainty. This is exactly the tack that the enemy wants the professed believer to take. The prince of the darkness of this world wants mankind to be comfortable with the shadowy places of faith. God requires certainty of faith which demands that the believer come away from the shadowy into the full light of Truth. It is only in the pure light of Truth that the power of God is released mightily to do the amazing in the life of the faithful.

The power of God is best displayed in the season when the flesh is at its weakest. It is when the flesh has been emptied of pride and boasting that the divine spirit has ample room to work mightily in the life of the believer. It is when everything has been offered up on account of love for God and there is nothing more to give but one's heart that the gates of Providence are fully opened. Only when this becomes the case, does the believer enter into the arena of strong faith. All things borne of faith are given freely. But there is a test of faith before each victory is garnered. It has to be that way so that there is due accountability and no doubt as to the source of the help.

The believer who aspires for strong faith has to be fortified with the meat of the spirit. The meat is garnered from the word of Truth that the believer feeds on as he seeks after Christ. It is embodied in knowledge communicated within the spirit as the believer matures in faith. It is embodied in that communicated through the medium of the Holy Ghost as information given from the divine throne to help the believer overcome that which stands in the way. It is embodied in the information given on a need to know basis to help fill out the missing elements in the believer's understanding of the Divine. It takes the meat of the spirit to bring both the seen and the unseen into sharper focus so that the harmony within creation can be ascertained. It takes such to inoculate against the surreptitious in the way so that the believer can perform marvelously as the Holy Spirit leads him. Spiritual meat affords intimacy with the Divine and avails uncommon wisdom to help the faithful do the marvelous in life. It is the meat of the spirit that makes for certainty of faith and sustains those that ride the passage way of light that connects Heaven and earth.

Chapter Highlights

- ✓ The journey to meet up with Christ passes through a place of blessed quietness that can be unsettling.
- ✓ The place of blessed quietness is where the faithful is uplifted in spirit by the use of wings of prayer.
- ✓ The walk of faith is a choice between peace through Christ or contention in the world.
- ✓ The anointing gained from baptism in the fire of Truth infuses certainty to the words of the faithful.
- ✓ The faithful that has passed judgment in the fire of Truth is given to bring light into darkness.
- ✓ The misguided sadly think that he that has acquired the most material has won life's top prize.
- ✓ It takes strength of character forged in the crucible of faith in God to live contrary to the world's way.
- ✓ Feigned spirituality is used to hide mankind's misdeeds and is a thin veneer that soon wears out.
- ✓ The spirit of God works mightily to change a man of many weaknesses into the virtuous and valiant.
- ✓ Although considered wise by many, to hedge on betting with God is really an act of foolishness.
- ✓ It takes spiritual meat gained by Truth to be transformed to come into harmony with Creation.
- ✓ Rejection of fame and fortune on account of love for God inoculates the faithful against evil.

The surreptitious wields an evil streak

With undercurrents to tow man down

In emotions ever as fickle as the wind

To flood the mind with passing fancies

Chapter 7

LOVE THAT ASKS FOR LITTLE

Grace is borne of goodness sake from love that asks for nothing in return and may be likened to the lifeblood that sustains the body of Christ. On the other hand, mercy is provision availed to the body of Christ by a 'Grand' entity outside of the fellowship but connected to it in spirit. Put simply, the body is nourished within by grace but provided from without by mercy. It is within the framework of grace that believers are sustained during spiritual immaturity and that of mercy that they ask to receive in maturity.

Wherever there is lack of grace, the body is devoid of the spirit of new life in Christ. Such a body is spiritually dead but plods along under the weight of the old self through a process of fission or self-cannibalism where the parts of the body devour each other. It is a hotbed of self-defeating activities that ends in spiritual death. It may look like a feast to the blind in spirit but it is really the macabre dance of maggots in a celebration of the dead and dying. By contrast, wherever grace abounds the body is filled with the spirit of new life. It is alive and abounds fully by a process of fusion where parts reach out to each other in cross pollination to create new life. It is a joyful feast not of eating and drinking in the flesh but of thriving in a spirit of goodness. It is indeed a life of milk for therein the new is borne and sustained. It is of honey as well because the parts fuse in love to produce the sweet nectar of new life.

The life that lacks grace makes itself evident in many ways. He that lacks grace has difficulty in giving thanks and showing appreciation. He is always on the defensive and cannot ask for forgiveness easily. He is wise in his own eyes and cannot ask for or welcome good counsel. He is prone to blaming and finding fault with others. He is easily provoked and lacks peace within. He is righteous in his own eyes and given to manipulation so as to win the approval of others. He does his 'good deeds' only when there is an audience to laud him with praise. He may be a professor of faith but he is not a true confessor for he feels exposed in pure light of Truth. He is a purveyor as well as a victim of such lies that masquerade as Truth. Beyond all that, such cannot perceive the 'hidden' things of God for he is a blind man that plods along in a world of darkness.

Wherever the true word of God is faithfully shared is a table of true enlightenment. It is a feeding trough where the sheep of the flock are nourished with the word of life. The word shared and laid out for the flock in Truth is good nourishment for the spirit. He who feeds worthily will be transformed in light of the spirit of the words that he has received in good faith. He that receives in good faith will lay up the words in the treasure chest of his heart. What one eats becomes him or one becomes what he eats. Either way, he will grow in the spirit of God or the spirit of God will grow within him. In the same vein, the follower after Christ will apprehend him or Christ will apprehend the faithful follower in due time. In time there will be no distinction between the two for the seeker will become an organic 'representation' of the spirit of God. He will become an embodiment of the spirit of God to always speak from the abundance of that which is laid up in his heart. In that case, the heart has become a holy place from which Truth is faithfully offered up in loving faith.

Wherever there is Truth, the light of God shines brightly. Being in the light of God brings about an enlightenment that cures spiritual blindness. When spiritual blindness is cured sight returns and one can see which way to go. He who knows which way to go is no longer 'lame' for he can then go freely on his merry way. The power and mystery of Christ is made possible with a healthy dose of grace. He that embraces Truth in love will be duly filled with grace. Where grace abounds is where the Spirit of God abounds also. The faithful that abounds in grace will be shielded from the traps of the prince of darkness. But he that has rejected Truth has not made room in his heart for grace to abound and for the spirit of God to find welcome. He will lack the wherewithal necessary for victorious living and will not be able to escape entrapment by the enemy. Grace is necessary for victorious living in the world and is availed to the seeker through the light of Christ. It is only through Christ that answers can be found to overcome the world and reconnect with the heavenly Father.

He through whom Truth is declared to reveal the hidden has become an exalted spiritual being. In effect, he has become an oracle through whom God speaks to mankind. Every oracle of God has been equipped as a precious vessel dully fitted to serve God and humanity in love. Through this calling on his life, such is given to impact many lives and change surroundings through the light of Christ infused in his words. Oftentimes the burden feels heavy and the work seemingly overwhelming but he that is truly called will always finds strength to carry on. It is in this light that the oracle of God diligently tends the earthly garden that God has appointed for him for therein is his victory ordained. Every such gardener is given to make the world better as he changes the human landscape with his words so that light may spread to help beclouded eyes.

Every true vessel of God is called to model a better way for the people whose eyes tradition has clouded. The way of tradition is surreptitious in that it aims to boast and vaunt self. But the new way of Christ is truthful, does not exalt self and eschews boasting. Only God is honored and exalted in the new way of Christ. Christ takes mankind into a bright future whereas the old way of tradition returns him to a dark past. The old way is emblematic of the serpent which molts and covers itself with new skin yet remains the same within its unchanging ugly heart. It prides itself in material things to spawn a culture of thievery, misappropriation and unaccountability. It is a cesspool where might assumes to be right and the wrong seems so strong. Every vessel that serves God truly hates the way of the world that the faithless love. He hates it when the creature mocks his Creator with his hypocritical and pretentious ways. He hates it for he knows that it breaks God's heart as he sees his beautiful creation earth marred with such ugliness and disregard for justice.

The true vessel of God does not hate the people but the way of spiritual ugliness that they have chosen. He that serves God truly loves the people so much that he is willing to lay down his life to journey to the distant and foreign land of Truth. The essence of that foreign land is the good and perfect that brings fulfillment. Every true vessel is a custodian of divine gifts who returns to share in love with those hearts willing to receive. It is by the true vessels that misguided hearts in the darkest of places get a chance to partake in or at least have a taste of the glorious availed in divine light.

Such is glory that is not boastful but dignified in hushed

splendor. It is the glory of the flower in spring blossom. It is the glory of the bird that sings because it is free to live and love. It is the glory of the eagle that soars in its audacious hope to touch the sky. It is the glory of the morning dew that covers all things with the wet kisses of life. It is the glory that mortal man once knew but lost in a faraway place called Eden.

God affords his true vessels such glory and protects them through their earthly journey. Every such vessel is a lover of Truth and an emissary of light who is willing to suffer in love to serve God's purposes. As such, his handwork will shine with distinction for God uses every vessel to accomplish the works of glory. The heavenly Father who created all has anointed such vessels among all peoples.

Within each race, color, tribe and tongue is a true vessel so chosen and christened in divine light for the people. There is always one christened in true light that is woven from the fiber of the people's lowly Nazareth. It is so because God has made provision so that every man can have a chance to meet or have knowledge of the true. Sadly, most men will meet them but never come to know such chosen vessels for who they are. It is not on account of oversight by Heaven. It is on account of spiritual blindness that bedevils mankind borne out of not seeking after God sincerely and not fully embracing the light of Christ.

Oftentimes the chosen vessel of light may not be openly acknowledged for who he is and may not be fully aware of the transformation that he has brought about among the people. For that reason, he may think that he has failed in his mission of bringing true light to rid the darkness within the hearts of the people. However, some do come to know without a doubt that a man for all ages has been woven from the cloth of their lowly Nazareth. They will know that a noble spirit has been wrought from where nothing good was expected to come. Every such vessel is used to show the true way so that those that sincerely seek can find it but the journey is always long and wearying.

The honey is not tasted before or during the battle but after victory has been secured. And so, the testimony of every chosen vessel will be enduring for his way will come to be desired and sought after by the people long after his work is done on earth. Each chosen vessel has embarked on the long great journey to divine glory where Truth nourishes the soul and sustains the spirit. Such are travelers among an innumerable company of the exalted in spirit that encourage, whisper comfort to soothe troubled souls, and sound the necessary alarm in love.

God uses every chosen vessel to start a new branch in the family tree of the everlasting. He is chosen to raise a tribe of the God fearing and peace loving. Each vessel must not underestimate what God has purposed for his life. Many will follow in his trail to do mighty works in the name of Christ. Every one chosen in this light is given to rear up spiritual children who will stand on his shoulder to do great things. They will carry his mantle to be enabled to see in purer light and be uplifted to greater heights.

The mantle of Christ is a precious gift bestowed by the heavenly Father on every chosen vessel. The mantle focuses the light of the flame and protects the flame of love from being blown out by evil winds of the times. The mantle diffuses the light of the flame so that it can be easy on the eye of the seeker. The mantle enhances the clarity of light yet shields the eye from smoke. The mantle makes possible the transportation of the flame to where it can be of the most benefit. The mantle is divinely woven with threads of grace and covered with the pigment of mercy so that the light of Christ can be well-received. The mantle is what defines every true light for what it is and to crown it for what it serves. The mantle is that which cloaks the enlightened spirit in eternal glory. But the mantle of Christ has to be kept clean and cared for in good faith by faithful obedience to Truth and in patient love.

Chapter Highlights

- ✓ Grace is borne of goodness sake from love that asks for little as the essence of Christ.
- ✓ The man devoid of grace lacks the spirit of life but the faithful abound in it to thrive in goodness.
- ✓ The life that lacks grace is manipulative, self-righteous and always on the defensive.
- ✓ The believer that embraces and lives in accordance with Truth will be filled with essence of the Divine.
- ✓ The believer cured of spiritual blindness will escape entrapment to perceive the wiles of the enemy.
- ✓ The faithful through whom God speaks is a vessel prepared to serve humanity in faithful love.
- ✓ God chooses some so that those in the darkest of places can come to know the glorious and free.
- ✓ There are sons of light for every community but many never know them due to spiritual blindness.
- ✓ The testimony of the emissary of light endures to be sought after long after his earthly work is done.
- ✓ The divine mantle is a precious gift bestowed on the chosen to protect the flame of love within him.

Man that seeks after intimacy with the Divine

Must forget the injustice and hurts of the past

There must be no bitterness found in his heart

As it beclouds the mind to douse love's flame

Chapter 8

ENTRUSTED WITH THE KEY

The season of harvest has ripened for the vessels that live to serve and please God. It is the season of fulfillment for the faithful whose handiworks are well received above. Such obedient vessels that yield to walk in the way that the spirit of God leads now move from victory to victory for the day has dawned when there is great power availed to them to do mighty works. The day has dawned when one man can chase a thousand and when that which takes a thousand days to do can be done in one day. Those for whom this day has dawned do not trust man's judgment but depend on God for guidance, power and strength.

The spirit of God is readily present and his power amply available in this new day for every vessel that is pure of heart. Only those hearts purified in light through Christ who have forgiven past injustices done to them are worthy of use in this new day. Such will get to write a new script in life. The faithful seeker meets up with Christ in the future and not in the past. For that reason, every believer must forget the injustice that has been done to him. There must be no bitterness found in him for such beclouds the heart to dampen the flame of love therein. He must let go of the past for he seeks after a new life in a new place. He must leave vengeance and judgment to the God of justice whose timing is always perfect. The tribulations of the past serve to prepare and strengthen faith in God through Christ. The faithful seeker must keep his eye on the prize ahead for he that returns to the places of the past can neither meet up nor keep up with Christ. He that has met up with Christ gets to stand under the mercy of God. For that reason, he must remain in the instant for he has become a son of 'today' who must be ready at all times to answer God's call to service. All great things appointed to be accomplished through Christ take place in the future and not in the past which holds no stake under mercy.

Indeed, it should be noted by every seeker that Providence lies ahead for those that seek in Truth after Christ. Divine gifts can only be realized through Christ when mankind opens his heart fully to Truth. However it takes the spirit of God to induce mankind to open his heart to heed. He that yields to the impulse of the spirit in such moments will hear some hidden but convincing truth that God has set aside for him to receive. Such are words communicated in truth and love through the speaker but directed to pierce through the guard walls of the listener's heart to reach his spiritual core. There are made known so that the listener will have little doubt that God is trying to reach him. All who are entrusted with such hidden knowledge are shooters of golden arrows which never miss their mark.

The hidden truths are words of knowledge and insight needed to address every situation encountered in life so that the best outcome can result. Such are words used to turn lemons into lemonade or better yet water into wine. He that is able to receive such knowledge has received the means to overcome and be victorious in life. He will have the words to reach men's hearts and pierce even the hardened ones. In effect, he can break the stony heart with his words to plant the seed of Christ therein in good faith with love. It takes such to induce the man with the hardened exterior to yield and allow the good within to show forth. He that can be used in this way is one divinely equipped to uplift those flattened by life's troubles and help reshape them into vessels worthy of use by God.

The faithful that is privy to hidden truths is given to do the marvelous in the sight of men to the praise and glory of God. Such is a custodian of the key words that unlock life's knots. He is given to live the life of the mysteries in the way of Christ for he has been purified in the dew of Truth and covered with the mist of life. Divine wisdom will crown his life with eternity marked as his final destination. Such is one who takes little for himself for he knows that he is passing through to a better place and so has no need for much on earth. It helps to think of him as a ghost that passes through the night time of the earthly experience who leaves a trail of enlightenment that changes the landscape for better in his wake wherever he has been.

To whom much is given is one from whom much is expected and to whom much is committed from him much is required. He that receives the heavenly gifts must do so with thanksgiving to God who gives good gifts in mercy. Such must never neglect to share or remain humble for he is only a vessel used to render reasonable service to the Creator and creation. Without the humility engendered through thanksgiving, mankind is prone to become vain and consequently unfulfilled within. The faithful cannot afford not to be humble for it is a divine disposition. Humility is the precursor as well as an invitation to goodness and mercy. The word 'please' is crucial for keeping the fountain of grace open. Lack of appreciation or not showing thankfulness shuts off the fountain. The word 'please' maintains the right hand in good use and keeps it from withering. The word 'please' makes the possession of the good and perfect gifts to be expedient for such are received with the right hand of gratitude.

The gifts received from the heavenly Father must not be abused but used for good service. He that does so will receive even more but he that does not will be denied. 'Please' is a word revered by the honorable but it is a strange notion for the violator in spirit that desires to take by force. The good gifts are given freely by the Father but such are not free. The honorable knows that he has life and due knowledge because God allows it. He knows that he has possessions because God makes ample provision for him. He is content in such knowledge and therefore boasts not in self accomplishments but in Christ.

He that is privy to the hidden truths is given to plow with the full yoke of the oxen of Israel with thanksgiving to God always. He is given to walk in the fullness of the riches of God through Christ. He will be like one that carries the mantle to set ablaze the flame of Christ. He will be the spiritual son in whom the Father is perfected. The full blessing of Israel will rest upon him so that he will have power both with God and with men. The spirit of God will be readily present and divine power mightily available through him. The invisible hand of God will always guide him to perceive opportunities where other men see none. He will receive favors where others are denied and have access to the third that only the sons can have. The curse of the serpent will be lifted from wherever he treads and in whatever he touches for he has been sanctified in Truth.

He that has set his hands to plow in the kingdom of God must not look back. The spirit and power of God have an exceptional utility quotient that serves humanity in countless ways through all areas of life. Divine power has the limitless potential to make, break or change things for better in the life of the believer. God is not to be resisted but yielded to. His power cannot be conjured up but tarried for. He chooses the vessel that he deems to be worthy of use. He chooses the faithful that will not hinder but allow his purposes to be accomplished on earth. Divine power is given to overcome myriad obstacles but partial to the humble, meek and truthful.

He whom the spirit of God deems worthy to be used in this light is of immense service to Heaven and earth. But he must always seek to please God and not men. He must tarry for the spirit of God to prompt him to perform his reasonable service as one who dwells in the congregation of the just. The latter is for the pure of heart and therein divine illumination orders footsteps. There is always ample room in the congregation for all who are willing to trust and obey in good faith. There is little worry there but peace within for all who tarry to heed the Master in good faith. Such is a desirable place that only a few find as it is not for those who seek after the praise of men. Those who seek after the praise of men dwell in partial light and shadowy places where the spirit within is often famished.

The divine spirit is the auto pilot who sets the course for those that dwell under the peace and light of Christ. The course must never be changed by the faithful for it has been set on a pre-determined course. He that follows the pre-set course will come into the knowledge of all things for he walks on the golden trail where mankind is given to search out the hidden truths. Every believer is judged by what he knows and lives by. It is a sin to have knowledge of Truth and not obey same. Many have no knowledge of Truth and therefore know not what to obey. Indeed there will be many stripes for those who know and obey not but little for those who know not what they do. Divine wisdom and knowledge are availed freely but such come with responsibility as well as accountability.

There is always a surreptitious spirit sent by the prince of the darkness of this world to tempt the pure of heart that dwell in the light of Christ. The enemy knows that the pure of heart have loving and giving hearts with no guile to be found therein. And so, the prince of darkness comes to entrap the faithful with feigned love embodied in the seductive spirit. But it is the kind that poisons the water. It looks lovely on the outside but it is ugly within. It is darkness that masquerades as light to becloud the mind and corrupt the seed of the great things that God has in plan for the faithful. The latter must remain separated from that which defiles the vessel for there must be no unequal yoking in Christ as it hinders the work of light.

Only the few who partake worthily of grace are nourished and sustained in spirit to meet up with Christ. Only those that have met up with Christ receive the key of knowledge to be able to search out the hidden truths and mysteries of the kingdom. He that has the key will be tuned to hear and understand with clarity. He will see and perceive the true nature of all things. The words of scripture will be framed into pictures wherein he will find himself because he has been adopted into the family of God. Scripture is really about good news and hope of the everlasting for mankind through Christ. He that has met up with Christ has become a son as well as one who will see self and life reflected throughout the scriptures. The things concerning Christ will fit the profile of his life for the sons share a common template that remains unchanging through time.

The key of knowledge and true understanding is never given to the profane for such will abuse it. It is for the righteous before God who live not for self but in love for all. The key of knowledge unlocks the secrets of the kingdom and creation itself. It unlocks the secret of the plain and unassuming manna that sustains the weary traveler through adversity. It unlocks the secret of Aaron's rod that has an everlasting covenant with life. It affords the key to the possessor to untie many of life's problems that bedevil humanity. However he that is entrusted with the key must think kingly thoughts and take princely steps in his earthly journey for he is judged by a higher standard.

Chapter Highlights

- ✓ He that serves God faithfully is always victorious in life for the Spirit of God accompanies him.
- ✓ Hidden truths are 'whispered' into faithful hearts and are used to bring about needed changes.
- ✓ Divine wisdom affords knowledge to break the hardened heart and mold such into a vessel of God.
- ✓ The faithful always leaves a trail of enlightenment that changes the human landscape for better.
- ✓ The faithful receive heavenly gifts under mercy with due acknowledgements to God always.
- ✓ Grace is revered by the honorable but a strange notion for violators that desire to take by force.
- ✓ The blessed see opportunities where others see none and receive favors where others are denied.
- ✓ The potential of the power of God to make, break or change things for better has no limits.
- ✓ The Spirit of God sets the course and guides the steps of those that walk in the peace of Christ.
- ✓ Feigned love is used by the enemy to becloud the mind and forestall God's good plans for mankind.
- ✓ The seeker that has met up with Christ will see his life reflected through the words of scripture.
- ✓ The righteous before God live not for self but in love for humanity and goodness.

Humility is well-acquainted with the Divine

For it is the essence of life and the enduring

The humble will always be worthy of honor

For Heaven embraces and never resists such

Chapter 9

NEW GIFTS AND SKILLS

For all intents and purposes, the very young in faith may be likened to fish that have just been pulled out of the darkened sea of worldliness. If such remain obedient in Christ, they will go on to become like fish broiled in the fire of Truth. The broiled fish is the faithful believer who has been baptized in the fire of the spirit of Christ. He is one who has willingly offered up self as a living sacrifice in the way so as to come into communion with the Divine. He is the diligent seeker given to meet up with Christ and duly join the congregation of the sons of God. He will become a congregant of the living church of Christ with a passport into the kingdom of God. All who have this passport of life can fish other men out of the sea of the world on to the path of redemption in accordance with divine will.

He that has met up with Christ will come into profound knowledge of the ways of God and be enabled thereby to experience the Divine in remarkable ways. He will become privy to sacred knowledge revealed only in true light to those pure of heart. The sacred pertains to the mysteries by which the sons of God battle victoriously against spiritual wickedness and darkness in the world. The young believer that has been set on the path of redemption must continue thereon with due diligence. He must remain obedient to Truth so that he can grow into certainty of faith in due time to come into knowledge of the mysteries and power of God through Christ.

The early years of faith are the most perilous for the slopes up God's mountain are very slippery. It is highly necessary in that season to live true to the sincere milk of the word so that the young roots of faith can remain nourished. When the roots of faith are nourished and established, the faithful believer will grow from milk to be able to eat the meat of the word as well as experience rebirth in Christ. However there are myriad temptations and great trials to overcome before this can come about. Rebirth in Christ is availed through grace and fully realized as the seeker matures spiritually to stand before God under mercy.

Redemption of soul and salvation in eternity with God do not come by mankind's efforts but as a divine gift received freely through grace. The young believer must persevere through the difficult circumstances and trials of the early years so that he can meet up with Christ to realize redemption and salvation. He must forego much in the

New Gifts and Skills

way as necessary so that in time he may become a son that stands before God under mercy. All knowledge obtained in seeking after Christ remains invaluable and true for all times. Nothing is wasted in seeking after Christ for what precedes serves as the basis from which the new emerges. The more the believer learns and keeps of Christ is the more that he is transformed into divine likeness. At full transformation, he will become one with Christ as a son well prepared to serve God in true light for all ages.

He that strives to be faithful in his spiritual walk must be willing to lay down his life for others as called for it is what frames Christ. He must be willing to accept all who come to him in search of Truth. He must be willing to accept all such as his spiritual charge. It must be that way if he desires to be fully baptized in the fire of the spirit of God. The spirit of God will never depart from him that has been baptized in Truth. The latter cannot be reversed and the gifts associated with cannot be revoked. God will not repent or change his mind about the gifts that come with baptism in the fire of Truth. It may be withheld for a season such as dams and locks control the flow of a river. However it is eventually released to serve its purpose in accordance with God's purposes. He that has been baptized in the fire of Truth will duly pick up his life again in full flourish to be divinely led into the newer and better.

The believer that has been baptized in the fire of the spirit will awaken to a new reality in Christ. He will find that he has become a different creature from what he used to be. He must therefore resist the tendency to return to where and what he has left behind. He will be disappointed if he attempts to do that for he will not find satisfaction in it. But in time he will come to find that the glory of the new that is now available to him through God is far greater than that of the old which must be left behind. He must reach out and embrace his new life in Christ fully. He that has been transformed in this light needs time to understand his new reality. It takes time to understand the scope and full nature of rebirth in divine likeness. The scope of services available to the reborn is a lifelong odyssey of discovery for such will no longer do things by his might or power but in the spirit of God. His requests will become readily granted in mercy and his conversations will cease to be of the lowly and worldly but of the purer and heavenly.

He that has been baptized in the fire of the spirit is bestowed with clarity of mind that enables him to be in tune with creation. He will gain a sense of orderliness that will dictate to him where things around him should be and what purpose they should serve. It is this sense of the nature of things that leads the faithful to get rid of the cumbersome in life. He that has clarity of mind can search out the important that matters in his life and environment.

Such is the nature of the new awakening in Christ for it

New Gifts and Skills

brings better understanding in purer light and hope that makes much possible for the believer. He that has been awakened fully in this light will come to discover that he is able to do certain things exceedingly well. Such is the ability of divine power to induce special gifts that had not been demonstrated before to surface from within everyone that is reborn in divine light.

It takes some time for the reborn in light to realize and fully understand that divine power availed through Christ makes the ability to do many things possible. Such must take time to take stock of all the gifts and skills that the spirit of God has induced to surface through him. The gifts usually add up to point in a clear and definite direction for his life. All the gifts are components that assemble into a divinely appointed vehicle that will carry him through the rest of his life as he serves God and goodness. The time invested by the believer to pray and take stock of his life in this wise will be highly rewarding. It will allow him to be able to recognize the new direction in which God is leading him for he has embarked on the sweet ride to glory.

He that has been baptized in the fire of the spirit will find out that everything left in his life has a destined purpose. He will find that all that he needs in his new life has been provided for. It will amaze him to find that everything now works out for good for him. He must therefore strive for perfection in all that he does as life has become about the

New Gifts and Skills

spirit of God doing the marvelous to behold through him. He must leave no room in his life for the un-needed and un-necessary but make more room in his heart for the lovely that is of a good report so that the spirit reborn within him can flourish in glorious service.

With the awakening of new life in the faithful, he will come to better know the roles destined for all that 'flock' to his side. He will come to know what divinely ordained part each has to play within the fellowship of Christ. All who embrace their roles will flourish but those who reject same will be left out of the divine design. There should be no attempt to mix the old with new life in Christ. The faithful should not attempt to resurrect his old life. He should nail the door of his old life shut and stride boldly into the open door of his new life in Christ. He must resist the urge to patch his old life on to the new. The old and new lives are different entities that do not mix well and do not match. There are to be kept apart for God's blessing is never realized in discord or confusion. The divine blessings abound fully when all parts are in harmony. The wine of the new life in Christ takes some time for the taste to be acquired but it turns out to be gloriously sweet in the end. But it is sweetness and blessing only realized by those willing to go where God sends and to do as he commands.

True enlightenment comes about by faithfully feeding and living in accordance with God's word of Truth. The feeding should not only take place during the times of prayer and study. Every moment in life is an occasion to learn about God if the believer is tuned in spirit to hear. God uses everything and every moment to teach the faithful about his way. All who reach out for the word of Truth must feed worthily for it is offered in love. It is bread of life that duly turns into the meat of the spirit. It is the meat of the spirit that makes for strong faith and affords the key of knowledge. Where the true bread of the word is faithfully broken and shared, certain truths that had hitherto been hidden thereabouts will be revealed. Such knowledge is duly revealed from a spiritual realm beyond mankind's flesh in moments of divine inspiration to bring the faithful into a greater light of understanding.

Greater understanding lifts up mankind's spirit higher to a place closer to the heart of God. He that is lifted up there can see as well as know better in purer light. The uplifted in spirit will acquire a heavenly perspective and be able to hear the still small of the Holy Ghost that affords the faithful comfort. The Holy Ghost whispers from heavenly places into the heart of the faithful to affirm the spiritual connection between God and man. 'He' is given to bring due knowledge so that the faithful can be prepared as necessary to deal with every situation and circumstance that he encounters in life. It takes such knowledge to help make the hills low, fill up the valleys and straighten the crooked for the faithful. The words of the Holy Ghost issue forth from the throne of the heavenly Father and have great capacity to change things for better as there are given to ameliorate life's circumstances. The words must be heeded once received as circumstances are changed for good when such are taken to heart and acted upon.

The Holy Ghost can only be received by the pure of heart for 'he' brings knowledge that is not to be profaned or used for selfish gain. The words of the Holy Ghost will not accomplish anything unless it is acted upon. The Holy Spirit is the medium which enables action in the faithful believer. It takes the Holy Ghost in conjunction with the Holy Spirit for the believer to accomplish the works of glory. The lust for material things is a dense fog that beclouds the mind to tune out reception of the Holy Ghost while the lust of the flesh is a choke that hinders the flow of the Holy Spirit. In effect, hunger after materials and the lust of the flesh limits the effectiveness of the Holy Ghost as well as that of the Holy Spirit. He that is to be fruitful in the kingdom way must curb his appetite for both the flesh and earthly materials. Moderation in all things makes the spirit to abound and keeps God near but the lust after the worldly keeps all things divine out of hand.

Chapter Highlights

- ✓ The broiled fish is emblematic of the believer who has been washed and purified in the fire of Truth.
- ✓ Those that are obedient to Truth are given to experience divine power in profound ways.
- ✓ True knowledge remains invaluable and enduring as the preceding serves as the basis for the new.
- ✓ He that desires fellowship with the Divine has to lay down his life as called in service of humanity.
- ✓ It is a lifelong odyssey of discovery as the faithful find out the scope of services availed by the Divine.
- ✓ Baptism in fire of the spirit bestows clarity of mind that enables believers to be tuned to creation.
- ✓ The faithful that is baptized in the fire of the spirit will find everything in his life to have a purpose.
- ✓ The baptized in Spirit must strive for the perfect for God will use him to do things amazing to behold.
- ✓ The transformed in spirit must nail the door of his old life shut and stride boldly into the new.
- ✓ Enlightenment comes in flashes of inspiration to bring mankind into greater light of understanding.
- ✓ Greater understanding lifts up the spirit to afford mankind a heavenly perspective about all matters.
- ✓ Lust of the flesh is a dense fog that beclouds the mind to tune out reception of the Holy Ghost.

Man that knows not his true self will remain

A poisoned fountain and a weakened pillar

Who cannot withstand the onslaught of evil

And can ill-afford to have the precious in life

Chapter 10

A STANDARD OF REFERENCE

The prayer of the righteous before God does much good to make situations better because such will always be heard. The righteous before God has been weighed and favored in the balance of divine judgment. As a result, he is a standard of reference by which the heavenly Father judges his fellows. He is a living candle held up by the Divine for others to observe and receive sight by. God entrusts the power of judgment to such that walk in the light of Truth shares in love with all. He that is entrusted with power in this wise has become God's proxy through whom forgiveness can be obtained for the penitent transgressor. Such are empowered to bind darkness on earth, release the lovely from Heaven, pray for life for the dying and bring healing to the believer in his wake. Such are the sons of Heaven given to the people as 'Christ' arisen or the chosen christened in light to walk among them. But every proxy of the Divine has to be perceived and received as such for the power that he brings to benefit the people.

A Standard of Reference

Whenever a Christ is given to the people, there will be another that will rise to make a false claim. The latter is a wolf in sheep's clothing that the people will follow. He will be held in high regard by the people but the true Christ will be esteemed lowly by them. In time God will exalt the true Christ beyond measure and the false will be known for the counterfeit that he is. The true Christ knows in the light of the future whereas the false Christ knows in the darkness of the past. The false Christ is a messenger borne out of the heart of darkness to take the people back to their misguided past. He takes them back into the captivity of a past that binds them in guilt, recriminations, greed and an insatiable hunger for more. He takes them back into the heart of darkness to a life of plundering and tearing apart where might assume to be right. He offers them the wisdom from below in a feast of strife, envy, jealousy, confusion and evil works. His ways beguile the people into a coffin as he cleverly frames his words to be that of tradition and the forefathers.

Whenever the heavenly Father anoints a Christ for the people, the people will invariably anoint a false one for themselves. Through it all, the true Christ will not protest for he knows that God cannot be mocked. He knows that time is the great equalizer that reveals the true nature of all things. He knows that it is by this seeming travesty, which is allowed to happen by God for good reason, that the truly anointed is rejected to be 'hung' on the cross to to the shame of the people. Unbeknown to them however, by their rejection of the true one in their midst, the people offer up the only sacrifice acceptable to God to avail them redemption. Although the people crucify the true ones in hatred yet such willingly accept to suffer on their behalf in love. Mysteriously, it is by crucifixion of the honorable one in their midst that a transition from the heart of darkness into the womb of light comes to take place among the people. It is by the crucifixion of the honorable before God that the eyes of the people come to be opened to glimpse the divine and come into knowledge of the true.

Crucifixion may appear to be daunting but it is a special platform. It is God's ultimate trump weapon used to bring down entrenched darkness for it is the cradle of divine justice. Within its seeming hopelessness lies the divine crucible which ejects the golden dust that confers immortality of soul on mortal man. He that is crucified on account of Truth soon becomes the living temple of God laden with the seeds of the glorious laden within. The honorable sacrificed on the altar of Truth dies in his old nature but rises again in a new self to the amazement of the people. With the crucifixion and resurrection in divine spirit of the honorable one, a curious thing begins to take place among the people. The power of wickedness and evil will begin to weaken and crumble among them. By the wrongful crucifixion of every true one worthy of honor, justice is given a new birth in a place where it has long been forgotten or never been known. Peace will awaken from its deep slumber to reappear as a long lost friend that has been sorely missed and in the same vein the little that comes with contentment will come to be chosen over the large that comes with envy and strife.

Mankind always rejects the just for his way of life is a mirror of indictment in which the people's injustices and wickedness are exposed. Mankind rather chooses one who may be a thief and robber in the ilk of 'Barabbas'. They would rather embrace him who regurgitates the old and takes them back to a past that should be forgotten. The false 'Christ' is an opaque mirror in which the people can never see their ugly ways. It may be convenient and comforting not to be confronted by one's ugliness but it is not expedient for knowing true self. He that does not know his true self will never be free in spirit. He will forever be a poisoned fountain and a damaged pillar. He will not afford the fulfilling and enduring availed through the Divine. The false 'Christ' is accepted because his way is convenient for the people and validates their unrighteous ways but sadly such keeps mankind bound in an ugly past.

The true one anointed by God but rejected by the people is a mirror in which all who are lost may find true self. He is a beacon divinely fitted to show the way to the future in the light of Truth and in love. Such is a fountain of living water and a strong pillar by which many afford the fulfilling and enduring. He embodies the Truth rejected because it is inconvenient and exposes the ways of darkness. It takes bravery of heart to walk in the way of light where Christ is found. He that follows the way of light to meet up with Christ is not only certain of faith but brave of heart as well. It takes the bravery of the lion to follow after Christ for the road leads from the familiar into a strange new place. The portion of Christ is offered as the new different from the old. It is portion reserved for those reborn in new spirit as sons of light to usher in the fulfilling and enduring. The reborn in the light of Christ is a son of mercy to whom blessings are tendered from above. He is availed the tender mercies of Heaven because he serves God and humanity as a willing sacrifice acceptable for the sins of many. He receives because he is a giver and shares in love with everyone that desires sincerely. Such is the nature of true love much honored above and that which defines every one divinely elected for the people.

God's elect for the people is often despised and resented by them for he is accused of subverting the established ways. He is seen as the strange upstart who aims to change the ways of the forefathers and ancestors. Yet it is of little concern to the people that the old way leads to envy and strife. It is of no concern to them that it is filled with lust and insatiable greed. It is of no concern to them that it devilishly triggers negative responses in mankind. He that champions the old ways is a cave dweller and a bat without sight. Sadly, the blind resists change the most for such are accustomed to 'caves' and will not dare to step beyond their comfort zone. But beyond the cave is the place of light and the refreshingly new. It is a new vista that unfolds as far as the eye can see laden with the blossom of hope. The elect comes to give sight to the people so that they can dare to step into the light where the future lies and all things become possible.

The elect for the people never casts about on his own but heads in the direction that the spirit of God leads. Typically he is led down a new path that the people had not trodden before for he is a breaker of new grounds where the fruitful trees of righteousness will thrive. He has been chosen as an agent to help rid the people of the residue of darkness entrenched deep within the heart. Darkness within the heart is often masked with smokes and mirrors but it is a pile of human defecation that stinks to the high heavens. It is for this reason that the elect is sent to model a new way of life much higher and desirable than that which the people have hitherto known. The elect model a new way so that the ravenous will no longer make chattel of their fellows.

God's elect embody the purest of hearts who have met the acceptance of the heavenly Father to be adopted into the divine fold. Every elect one comes as a bearer of true light and to demonstrate the heavenly way to the spiritually blind. Such are to be found in every community on earth.

A Standard of Reference

They may be sundered far and wide but are knit together in spirit with the golden threads of life spun from the fiber of Truth. It is the heavenly Father that makes this glorious quilt of different colors, tongues, and cultures to portray the same picture of Christ individually and collectively. It is a quilt that embodies the sun of righteousness. It has arisen in every land so that mankind everywhere may come to know and see that the word of God is forever true for all peoples. Christ has come to full life in many hearts in diverse places as a world wide web that is connected in Truth and pulses with life as well as love. Many are able to perceive and know the true elect anointed for them yet many more are still enchanted by the wiles of the false ones in their midst. He that has rejected Truth will never know the true but flounder in spiritual blindness.

Many in the world have been prepared and readied in spirit to bring about the glorious as new things borne of the old. The faithful that walk in the light of Christ are given to do the marvelous in the sight of men. Mankind's heart has to be right in order for his walk to be righteous. Footsteps will always be in right places at right times where the heart has embraced Truth. The marvelous to behold are the works by which God bestows divine glory on the sons of light. These are the works by which the sons withdraw from the treasures that they have laid up in Heaven. The sons partake of the heavenly and share in the light of Truth and love with all as due through Christ. The spirit of God is only effective where truth, grace and peace abound. The spirit of God will not deceive or lie and by the same token cannot be deceived. The divine spirit avails gifts that must never be profaned, abused or exploited for selfish gain. 'He' is given from the exalted heights so that the earthly and lowly can be uplifted in spirit to perceive God's kingdom of light.

He that has strong faith and great vision to trust God fully will always do work that men will come to praise after the passage of due time. He may be misunderstood while he does the work for the spirit of God leads in new ways and does new things. The new thing is often unknown and initially disparaged but appreciated later. It takes time to become used to the taste of the new. He that is to be used for the works of glory through Christ must not look for praise while his labor is afoot. He that looks for praise of men while the work is being done will find it hard to do the righteous for such is a cross-current that carries away from the direction that God leads. The true laborer seeks not after such praise but stays the course that God has ordained for him. It is only thereby that God will secure victory for him to enjoy the honey after the battle is done.

Chapter Highlights

- ✓ The righteous have passed judgment to become the standard of reference by which God judges all.
- ✓ Wherever there is one that knows in true light, there will be a false other that knows in darkness.
- ✓ The sacrifice of the innocent unleashes power that gives justice a rebirth where it has been forgotten.
- ✓ Mankind rejects the just for he is a mirror of indictment in which injustice is exposed.
- ✓ Every elect one is a mirror in which the lost earmarked for redemption may find themselves.
- ✓ The elect one is despised and resented for he is accused of changing the old and established ways.
- ✓ Every elect one is ordained to be a breaker of new grounds where trees of righteousness can thrive.
- ✓ New life in Christ knits all peoples together with the threads of life spun from the fiber of Truth.
- ✓ Victory borne of the cross has been replicated over the world among all cultures, nations and peoples.
- ✓ The new man of light is ordained by the heavenly Father to inseminate others with the seed of Christ.
- ✓ The heart that embraces Truth will have footsteps guided to be in the right place at the right time.
- ✓ The praise of men is a cross-current that carries away from the direction that God leads.

Humanity wins and no one is left without

When kindness and goodness rule the day

For thereby is the curse on the earth lifted

That sows enmity tween hope and harvest

Chapter 11

HEAVEN RECORDS ALL

Whether aware of it or not, life on earth is for mankind to prove his worthiness for company with the Divine. Earthly living is a proving ground of the inner man in the fire of Truth. In essence, earthly living is a test of how faithfully each person lives by Truth. The faithful and true remain unwavering whether in the little or grand. Given that no one can ever be perfect with regards to Truth, there is however an acceptable threshold for passing judgment. It is much like the purification of gold where an assay of ninety percent is a desirable minimum threshold.

Both the faithful man who fears God and the faithless that does not must pass through this fire of Truth. The faithful may be brindled on the outside by it but he will remain untouched in the inner core of the spirit. To be brindled on the outside is to suffer material loss as well as the world's hatred for embracing Truth. On the other hand, the faithless may appear to be untouched without but he will be totally scorched within in his inner core where it matters most at the end of the day. In today's world, many may appear to be untouched on the outside on account of their possessions but are indeed scorched and empty within with nothing of value to God.

For the faithful in Christ, it turns out that passage through the fire of Truth is necessary for baptism in the Spirit of God. It takes baptism in the fire of Truth to remove the entanglements of worldliness which ties up mankind's soul to keep him earthbound. The worldly drag down and must be removed first before that which lifts the soul upward can be afforded room to take its place. Truth is much like living water that flows from the throne of the Almighty God to nourish mankind's heart. Fire cannot burn Truth for it is permeated and soaked in the certainty of living water. On the contrary, fire burns the untrue because it is hollow dry chaff bereft of living water.

The world of today is a place of the false and untrue filled with intrigue and caprice where many perish for lack of true knowledge. Mankind no longer feels obligated to live up to his promises or act true to his words. Many are easily beguiled and misled on account of this prevalent spiritual malaise. But those that love Truth are not so easily misled for they are be able to perceive in true light. He who does not love Truth has made no room for divine light to govern his life. Rather he has made himself blind and given room to the spirit of the darkness of the world to dictate his life

The spirit of the world is a purveyor of the untrue often masked as Truth. He that is in league with it soon becomes a soul lost in darkness unwittingly prone to choose the false over the true.

He that loves Truth will have access to wisdom that comes from above. Wherever the wisdom of God is availed and duly welcomed is where the spirit of life comes to dwell. It is by the love of Truth that mankind comes to abound in light and be sanctified therein. Sanctification is when mankind faithfully lives by Truth so that divine light governs his life to afford him immunity from the darkness in the world. It is by this divine immunity afforded by Truth through Christ that the believer is able to reject and resist the untrue borne of the spirit of the world. The sanctified in Truth are not at home in this world for they know that the earth is not their final destination but a transit stop to a better place.

They that love Truth receive freely of God's wisdom in love and know not to profane but to use such for the benefit of all. He that receives in love from God is only a caretaker for God. He is called to use his gifts and possessions to make the world a better place. Therefore it behooves him to always give consideration to the impact of his decisions and actions on the welfare of humanity. He is called not be a wolf that is driven by the urge to have more and lives to take. Rather he is called to answer to the spirit that urges mankind to share with the needy and live in peace with all. The faithful in this light know that to be righteous before God, mankind must not just live for self. They know to treat others as they would like to be treated for all are created by the same heavenly Father. They know that God sees and records everything that is done on earth below from Heaven above and therefore live to please him. And so, they live in that greater love or charity that asks of mankind to live in sacrificial love so that no one is precluded from true knowledge and light of the Divine.

The faithless man lives for the praise of men and not for the approval of God whom he cannot see. Since God cannot be seen with human eyes, he reasons that the heavenly Father is not there to see him. Therefore he is often a good performer who does his so-called 'good' deeds in the presence and for the praise of onlookers. He that seeks out an audience to witness and praise him for his good deeds does not have true charity in him but is vain glorious. He puts on the semblance of charity so that he may be held in high esteem by other men. He is but a performer with an insatiable appetite within who wears a fake garment soon to be rags in his crave for the dust of earthly glory. He that is led by the spirit of the world to seek after men's praise is often beguiled into ill-advised 'undertakings'. Though his intentions may look good in the eyes of men, the seeker of men's praise is an undertaker of dead works who cares not for the welfare of humanity at large but is governed by self-interest. Such may be a master at staging good shows to bring him men's accolades but he will be left spiritually wanting.

Be that as it may, humanity has come into a reality check. The cosmic wheel has sped up and a separation of the true from the false is well underway. There are a chosen number, the people of God and the meat of the grain of humanity, who have been up lifted in spirit into the exalted realm of the Divine. These are the worthy before God who have embraced Truth and live in obedience to divine will. All who have embraced Truth to live in its light are now bestowed with knowledge from the treasure trove of divine wisdom. But those that have rejected Truth are precluded from this knowledge tendered in light and love through Christ. They are left out of God's will to flounder in the world's darkness. Through willful blindness, the faithless have chosen the broad and quick way that leads to spiritual dearth. Instead of doing right by God, they take his words for naught. They look for short cuts and feast on their fellow man for gain with no fear or love for God but lust in their hearts for all things worldly.

All who partake of true knowledge are soon transformed in spirit to realize new life through the teachings of Christ Jesus. Such that are transformed in that wise are led along an enlightened path that is in agreement with God's will to accomplish his divine purposes on earth. New life in the light of Christ affords release from the bondage of worldliness as well as protection from the winds of evil. He who has realized new life through Christ must secure his victory for the power of God is near to aid him. He is one that feasts in light with Christ Jesus as well as the other sons of God and has joined the congregation of eternal souls for whom the veil of the temple has been lifted up.

The feast of light that sustains the sons is wisdom and knowledge of the mysteries. It is by such that the faithful afford the key to access divine power. All who have a place at the divine dining table are given to partake in conversations in heavenly places. All who partake in this wise are members of the living church of Christ. These are to be found among all peoples of the earth and have power from God that flows from above through them. It takes such power to lead others into true light as well as heal those willing to receive in good faith.

All who feast with Christ are not only 'filled' with the spirit of new life but are duly remade in his spiritual image as the sons of light. Christ is the spirit of life as well as the Spirit of God made manifest in man. God makes much available to the sons of light for such are filled to the utmost with the Spirit of Christ. It takes the latter for mankind to afford the means to induce transformative changes within humanity. All who are filled with new life in this wise are divinely guided as catalysts that set in motion the regeneration of the earth in a heavenly order. It takes their intercessory prayers and love for mankind to inject measures of strong faith into the stream of human consciousness needed to hold the tide of wickedness at bay so goodness can abound. Every true son sacrifices freely as needed to bring about fundamental changes that redeem and add value to things on earth. They are also the tools used by the Divine to bring down spiritual wickedness entrenched in the 'high places' of the world.

The unceasing tides of wickedness continually gnaw at the fabric of humanity's soul and would overwhelm mankind easily without the intercessory prayers of the sons of light. The latter are matured in Christ and constitute the bulwark that resists the evil that pervades the world today. It is their prayers that make it possible for goodness to exist in the world as well as help stay the hand of divine judgment awhile. They are the few for whose sake God will delay the destruction of 'Soddom'. It is their constant prayers for forgiveness both for themselves and for others as well as their painful cries for justice that stir the divine heart to compassion.

The sons or the christened in light are spiritually purified beings that are certain of their place in God. Such know to live in true obedience to Truth so that there is no room left within for the enemy to hide. They love God with the heart, soul, mind and strength. When mankind loves God

In that wise, it opens up a new vista that is quite in contrast to that of the world. The new world opened up is the kingdom of God where the faithful enter to be able to do all things through Christ.

The kingdom opened up is for those who have been saved to keep spiritual companionship with the Divine. The christened in light being spiritually matured in Christ are reborn in spirit to begin life in this kingdom of light where God is sovereign. Up until spiritual maturity, the seeker dwells in the place of shadows. Like most others who seek after Christ, they dwell in a place that hovers between darkness and light. The latter is Dalmatia or the place of lesser light where most professed followers after Christ settle spiritually and never get past. Only the worthy before God can get past Dalmatia to become reborn in full light as sons. The seeker after Christ that is reborn into full light has gone beyond the flesh to join up with the sun of righteousness that shines light everywhere and into everything. He has finished the race of life victoriously to win the crown of life everlasting that attests to a life well-lived on earth to Heaven's approval.

Chapter Highlights

- ✓ New life in light through Christ is the anti-dote to the prevalent darkness in the world today.
- ✓ The believer who has been embalmed in Truth is immunized from the ravages of evil in the world.
- ✓ The righteous always consider the effects of their actions on the welfare of humanity at large.
- ✓ The unfaithful man misguidedly lives for men's praise but the faithful seek after God's approval.
- ✓ The righteous are the grain of humanity and have been uplifted in spirit into a purified state.
- ✓ The faithful believer is led by the spirit of life along a path that is in harmony with God's divine will.
- ✓ The prayers of the saintly inject measures of good faith into the world that holds wickedness at bay.
- ✓ The intercessory prayers and painful cries of saintly souls move Heaven to act in compassionate love.
- ✓ The believer that loves Truth will become certain in faith to have his spirit settle in God over time.
- ✓ The faithful that is reborn in Spirit will become a light that shines to make all situations better.
- ✓ The righteous have a universal spirit and treat all mankind as kindred borne of one heavenly Father.

That which sustains in darkness suffices not

When man is born from the womb into light

For the world without requires that man sees

To know where he fits and best role to play

Chapter 12

FROM WATER INTO LIFE

A commitment to fully live in obedience to Truth or the baptism of John as it is often alluded to is a pre-requisite for communion in spirit with Christ. The believer must first embrace and live by the words of Truth in good faith before he can begin to live in true light. It is through faithful living and obedience to Truth that the believer comes to be remade in the spirit embodied in God's words. The baptism of John is like the amniotic fluid that incubates the baby while he is in the mother's womb. He receives nourishment by it but nevertheless he is still in darkness for the womb is a dark place. His nutrition in the womb will help him in many areas of development but it will not help him to see for he does not need sight yet. He will need more than that which sustained him in darkness when he exits from the womb. The world of light is different from that of darkness. Therefore when mankind is born from the world's darkness into God's light he has to receive a different kind of nourishment. He has to receive nourishment that activates as well as strengthens spiritual sight so that he can thrive in the new world that awaits. It is in this wise that the young in faith are fed with the milk of the word in lesser light but the spiritually matured are nourished with meat of the word in greater light.

Obedience to Truth is very important in seeking after new life in the light of Christ. It is the process by which the residual and lingering areas of weakness in the life of the seeker are sorted to rid the flesh of the worldly so that the seeker can be sanctified or embalmed in Truth. To live fully by Truth helps to nudge the seeker spiritually to take a step back from worldly pursuits so as to step towards God. It works much like a check valve that keeps the polluted waters of the worldly out but allows living water in that sustains the seeker in new life in Christ. To live by Truth takes courage in that the seeker has to let go of the world's ways. It causes an apprehension or sense of foreboding as a dark cloud that duly passes to break in freedom of spirit and dawn of new light. The seeker may not be aware of it but the dark cloud portends baptism in spirit and rebirth into the greater light of the Divine. It is by baptism in spirit that mankind becomes an agent to bring about changes that transform humanity for better. It is by baptism in spirit that he becomes the herald of a new way of life and bearer of the new wine of Christ.

The breaking of the spiritual dark cloud over the life of

the believer is a signifier of release from the earthbound and the ushering into the heaven bound. It signifies the time to be reborn in the light of Christ as a son in the heavenly way. He that is reborn in that light will be connected to the three dimensions of the Divine. To be reborn in light affords mankind the ability to break through the barrier of complexity consciousness that encircles him and separates the mortal from the immortal. To be reborn in light enables the believer to finally overcome the worldly and join in spirit with the heavenly. It is after the dark cloud has broken into the light of the new that the crown of thorns and mockery of the world which every true believer wears on account of love for God turns into the golden crown of life. The reborn in light is irreversibly changed in spirit and there can be no going back for him. He emerges from this spiritual change with an urgency that seeks to show forth that which has risen in him. Such becomes divinely charged with the spirit of Christ and committed to the business of winning souls to the heavenly way as life's true calling. The spirit charged into the reborn in light can be perceived by those that hunger after righteousness and welcome Truth for such has become a host of Christ come back to life within.

That which dwells and shines forth from the reborn in light is knowledge and wisdom from the heavenly throne given to afford mankind reconciliation with the Creator. The reborn bring a message from a heavenly perspective infused with a sense of urgency that pleads with all to embrace Truth and put their spiritual house in order. It is message that reminds those willing to embrace that time has come for all to stand up to be measured for God has brought out the yardstick by which to do so. The reborn in light is the yardstick by which God measures those around him to show each his short-comings. Those who have been earmarked will respond in good faith and change their ways for better. But for many others the message of hope will always ring hollow and its appeal of little effect.

The hallmark of the reborn in light is adoption as sons of the heavenly Father. The sons and the Father need to be in spiritual agreement always for divine power to abound and flow mightily. The Father is the generator, the Son is the transformer, and the Holy Spirit is the power that does the work. None can be of great effect without the other. Wherever the will of the Father and the son are in agreement is where divine power shows forth mightily to do the marvelous for mankind to behold. He whose will is always in agreement with that of the Father is one given to be 'christened' in light. Divine power is manifested fully through the believer after christening in light for thereafter both Father and son are in agreement always.

Enmity between the son and the Father is the choke in the transmission of divine power. The enemy knows this and plots to put a wedge between Father and sons. Enmity between the two chokes off the power which infuses new life into all things to prevent the onset of spiritual death. Therefore there must be reconciliation between the sons and Father before the future can be truly ascertained to be secured. Enmity between Father and sons creates an uncertainty that beclouds the future. Uncertainty results from the fruit or union of the good and evil. Certainty is borne of goodness or agreement with the will of the Father and affords mankind the ability to realize the fullness of divine riches. It is only by certainty of faith that mankind can resume the intimate times that he once enjoyed with God that was interrupted ages ago in Eden.

The reborn or 'christened' in light are the sons who model that reconciliation between Father and sons which must be aspired for. Christening in light comes about when the seeker has given all and seems to be on his last spiritual legs. Although this is the moment of his victory he will harbor ill-conceived thoughts about being abandoned by God. To his dismay he will seem to be trudging alone and forgotten. To make matters worse, the enemy will enter the fray. Being a master at masquerading as an agent of light, the enemy will show up to promise companionship and rewards for the seemingly abandoned seeker. But it is all really a ruse devised by the prince of darkness to entrap the seeker after Christ into a downward spiritual spiral. It is precisely at this moment of seeming hopelessness that the new man of Christ steps out from within the seeker to lead the way and urge him forward. He that steps out from within the seeker after Christ is the christened in light. Amazingly out of the old uncertain self, the seeker has been reborn as a son of light certain of his place in God. Thereafter the reborn will never walk alone for he will always have a divine vehicle at his disposal to aid him as he keeps his appointed round on earth. The enemy of light and mocker of the believer will also be a witness in this grand moment. He will know to honor and keep safe distance from the christened who has overcome him.

When the inner man of Christ steps out from within to lead the way and urge the faithful forward is when he must dare to take his place among the mighty before God. He must wake up to his new reality as a son of Heaven who cannot be touched by the prince of darkness. Therefore there is no moment left for him to waste. He must become forthright in his declarations of Truth to all and be bold in his actions. Being one reborn in divine light, the sun of righteousness has arisen in him so that he is able to walk in light always in a dark world. He is able to perceive and have insight into the true nature of things in all situations so that he can resist evil and make goodness to abound on earth. It is in this light that the Holy Ghost is availed so as to keep the reborn in light well informed.

He that walks in the light of Truth is guided by the tweets of the Holy Ghost. Such no longer has to lean on his own understanding for he has received a steadfast companion who will never let him down. The information received by the Holy Ghost not only comforts but brings illumination and clarity into every situation. Without the information and timely updates availed by the Holy Ghost, the christened is liable to stumble in a dark deceitful world. Although the christened in light walks in a dark world with wisdom informed from above, he is called to show compassion for the spiritually blind. All who dwell on earth that are not tuned to the Holy Ghost are susceptible to being deceived. They will fall for any of the myriad ploys of the prince of darkness for lack of knowledge in true light. Such never know better and inevitably live a life style that fits into the world around them. They will continue to live by lies, half-truths and denial of Truth as they try to keep up appearances with the world but become further estranged from God. The estranged is not well-informed and mistakes the fake for real so that the true that he should hold dear to heart becomes neglected or discarded.

To be spiritually estranged from God is to never know divine or greater love. Where love for God is absent, one cannot truly love himself or another. Ability to realize divine love starts when mankind has goodness in his heart and lives with love for all. Only then can he spiritually grow to love Truth and thereby come to love God as he should. Where one does not love Truth or have fear for God, love will not abound in his heart. In that case, it is hatred for brother and darkness that will come to take root in his heart. All who are faithful in light after Christ cannot help but have love for others even though they may be hated by many. Hatred of brother blinds the spiritual eye so that mankind cannot perceive in divine light. Sadly the spiritually blind fail to appreciate life's blessings as should or honor the sacrifices made on their behalf by others.

Whether one is aware of it or not, all men are combatants in the struggle of love over hatred, light over darkness, hope over despair and life over death. Willful ignorance results from the rejection of Truth and leads many to unwittingly battle for the enemy to their demise. The battle field of faith is littered with needless casualties because many fail to realize that the fight between light versus darkness is not to be taken lightly. It is really about life and death. Countless souls have been lost in battle to the enemy because they lacked sufficient knowledge needed for victory. They failed in the fight against evil because they lacked due guidance and spiritual fortitude to persevere through life's challenges. They lack such because they fail to obey God's word or honor Truth. But those that obey Truth always abound in that needed for victory for they walk in light in a world of darkness.

Chapter Highlights

- ✓ A sense of foreboding hangs over the faithful believer before he is reborn in divine light.
- ✓ The crown of thorns and mockery that the faithful wears duly turns into the crown of eternal life.
- ✓ The faithful must put his spiritual house in order to be deemed worthy to receive the enduring.
- ✓ There must be reconciliation between the Father and sons for divine riches to abound fully.
- ✓ The matured in spirit must be bold in words and action for he has power to change humanity.
- ✓ Only the matured in spirit can bring enlightenment and healing that many in the world sorely need.
- ✓ Without the certainty afforded by the Holy Ghost, man is left with the delusion of self-righteousness.
- ✓ The faithless that lacks the Holy Ghost will fall for the deceptive ploys of the prince of darkness.
- ✓ The prince of the darkness of this world harbors special hatred for those reborn in light after Christ.
- ✓ All are combatants in the struggle of love over hatred, light over darkness, and life over death.
- ✓ Mankind can only pass from death to eternal life when he has learned to live in love with his fellows.

Truth condemns not the creature

But helps man to perceive in light

So he can receive freely from love

And feed from the Creator's bowl

Chapter 13

ASSURANCE OF THE FAITHFUL

The way of Christ is about caring and sharing. It calls for the faithful to make voluntary and selfless sacrifices in love that benefit others in the light of Truth and in accordance with God's will. It is by such sacrifices that many come to afford divine gifts as well as have goodness abound on earth. It is by such spiritual gifts availed in the light of Christ that new life is infused in people and situations. He who gives the spiritual which brings life rather than the material which is bereft of it is a courier of the divine. Many in the world can give the material but only a few can afford spiritual gifts to share with others. The material is not only short lived but has the tendency to corrupt the soul as mankind is often obsessed with it. However spiritual gifts shared in love through Christ infuses new life into humanity to make it collectively better.

Every gift shared and nurtured through Christ evokes the light that leads mankind closer to the Divine. He that has been led to the Divine will be blessed in countless ways for he has come into the arena where mankind is perfected in love. He will garner Godly attributes and his prayers will be readily answered for he will know what to pray for. He will abound in every area of life for he is like one that makes withdrawals from that which has been deposited for him in the heavenly vault under safe guard. One of the special gifts availed to the faithful is that of spiritual perception. It is the third eye availed to the faithful through Christ to help make all things bare so that he can be well informed about things that matter. The believer bestowed with the gift of spiritual perception is one that will always walk in true light and have his footsteps divinely guided.

The gift of spiritual perception is divinely availed so that mankind can be able to discern the good from the bad, the real from the fake and the true from the false. Spiritual perception is necessary for victorious living in this world of 'wolves masked in sheep's clothing'. It removes or at least minimizes such fears that the believer may harbor in a predatory world for it protects him from the wiles and traps of the enemy. Spiritual perception affords greater illumination and is bestowed on the pure of heart that live for all and not for self. Such is the means by which the faithful come to see all things in true light and no longer in shadows. It is the seeing-eye companion that helps him who would otherwise be spiritually blind to navigate through life without slipping on its treacherous slopes or sliding over its slippery terrain.

Assurance of the Faithful

The gift of spiritual perception gives much comfort and assurance to the faithful believer. It reinforces his belief that there is an eye in the sky that keeps track of evil and wickedness to alert him of encroaching danger. Spiritual perception is not only a lifesaving gift but a game changing one as well. It is the reason for the courage of the faithful and the assurance of the hopeful. This highly treasured gift lets the faithful know that he is not alone but that God is with him always. He whose heart is set after the pursuit of the materialistic cannot receive this gift for it is only for the noble in spirit. It is given to all who are noble in spirit and live in the true light of Christ as protection against the wicked devices of an evil and capricious world.

The gift of spiritual perception is divinely availed to those who care for humanity's common welfare. It is for the shepherds of the flock whose spirits dwell in the bowel of mercy. The latter is for the receiving and passing on of divine gifts so that those who lack may be nourished. Spiritual perception affords necessary insight to those that dwell in the bowel of mercy so that they can change situations and people for better. This useful gift is availed not to judge or condemn mankind but to help enlighten minds by sharing Truth in true and loving light. But yet the sinful man always feels uncomfortable and exposed in the presence of Truth. For that reason, shame often compels him to avoid and shy away from the corrective mirror that the spiritually perceptive hold up in true light.

However those who welcome such Truth will bask in its light to have many areas of weakness in their lives changed for better. The gift of perception helps to shine light into the dark recesses of men's hearts so that the love of God may be allowed in to dwell therein. Truth can never be silenced where there is good news to be shared and evil to be denounced. The light of God shines brightest and the voice of Truth speaks most boldly in the midst of darkness where the spirit of death lurks. The unfaithful may not be receptive to it initially but Truth never returns void for it always finds the mark to leave an imprint on the soul. Every soul that is divinely earmarked to receive Truth will do so and come to know the heavenly Father in due season. With the passage of time, all men for whom God has reserved a place in his kingdom of light will awaken in spirit to be led therein. They will come to fully realize and bear testimony to the redeeming power of Truth shared in love through Christ.

The heavenly Father has good intentions for mankind. However the unbelieving soul will never know the contentment that comes with the good and perfect gifts that God avails mankind in love through Christ. Such who have set their hearts on the desires of the world can never experience true fulfillment but will always have lack in the spirit within. They may experience passing moments of happiness but never the true joy that comes from the love and knowledge of God. Unbelief leads mankind into the sinful life and sin leads mankind into ungodliness. The ungodly man resists Truth even though same is necessary for mankind to have healing and wholeness in life. Be that as it may, it needs to be noted that it is not the sinful man that resists Truth but the spirit of darkness discomforted by light that lurks within him which does.

He that shares the word of Truth is called to do so with compassion for many are spiritually blind. He must share with love and for the goodness of humanity. He is not to do so for material gain but out of love and in obedience to God's will. Although he labors not for material gain yet Providence will always attend to bless him for his good deeds on behalf of fellow man. The sower of the word may speak discomforting Truth but it does the discomforted much good in the end. The true sower speaks about that which has been laid in his heart by the Holy Ghost. The latter enables and speaks through the sower so that those willing to embrace can have due knowledge and not falter. This spiritual intervention is always timely availed to help mankind cease from walking about blindly on earth. Without the undergirding of the spirit, the burden of God's Truth will be too heavy for man's flesh to carry and the deafening wax of the ear of the sinful impossible to pierce.

In as much as Truth often discomforts and makes the sinful feel condemned yet the word of God never intends to condemn mankind. It is the heart and conscience of the sinful that convicts him. Truth serves to bring light into darkness wherever it exists. It speaks to the heart in order to save mankind from the onslaught of evil around him and from spiritual death that stalks him. It speaks to save the soul from condemnation and to offer new life through Christ. Truth does not placate but shoots straight for it means to heal, free and bless. And so, he who is convicted by Truth must confess and seek forgiveness from God.

It takes the spirit of God both to convict and to free the sinner from guilt. He who has been freed by Truth will be empowered in spirit by same. God will hear his prayers and answer his petitions for his spirit will be able to soar to the heavenly heights. The spirit that freely soars upwards will duly come into communion with the Divine to become the certain who fears, serves and honors in truth as well as love. Such that is free in spirit has received the gift of redemption availed by grace through Christ. He will put God foremost and accept divine will as sovereign in life. If so ordained, he will receive salvation which is bestowed by God under mercy to those that he deems fit to be adopted into the divine household to join his eternal company.

Chapter Highlights

- ✓ The reborn in divine light can induce new life in people and situations to revitalize them.
- ✓ Spiritual perception enables the believer to walk in true light and have his footsteps guided by God.
- ✓ Spiritual perception protects the faithful from the wiles and traps of the enemy in a predatory world.
- ✓ The heart that is set after materials is precluded from the gift of spiritual perception.
- ✓ The gift of spiritual perception helps to expose darkness so truth and love can abound.
- ✓ The light of God shines even brighter in the midst of darkness where the spirit of death lurks.
- ✓ The heart set on the desires of the world will not know the contentment that comes with Godliness.
- ✓ It takes the undergirding of the Holy Spirit to lighten the burden of cross in the way of Christ.
- ✓ Truth speaks to the heart of sinful man in order to save but not to condemn him.
- ✓ The believer who puts God foremost in life will be duly changed to join with him in spirit in due time.
- ✓ Faithfulness asks of the man saved by grace through faith to lend his hand to help save another.

Discontentment is a spiritual malaise

That sadly afflicts many in the world

Leads to endless and insatiable crave

With desires that only fuel raging fires

Chapter 14

GREAT VISION AND STRONG FAITH

The faithful are duly motivated to share the word of Truth so that the spiritually blind can receive sight and the young in the way can be established in Christ. By his grace and goodwill towards mankind, God has made the word of Truth readily available to all through the teachings of Christ Jesus. All who are willing to embrace Truth in good faith can be awakened within to realize spiritual maturity duly in divine light and love. It is not God's intention to leave any deserving believer out of his plan for mankind but rather his desire is for his kingdom to be built up with as many faithful believers as are willing to trust him.

Although intentions may be good and the desire strong, the young in faith always struggle to allow necessary time for Truth to bear fruit. It is in this area that the Spirit of God works through grace to buttress the faith of new and young believers to overcome initial struggles. Some prevail over such struggles but sadly many others fail. In effecting redemption through grace, it takes the Holy Spirit to bring results to fruition as it pleases the heavenly Father. Man cannot choose or decide in this matter but be willing to obey and yield to God's sovereign will. However the heavenly Father will go to great lengths to find and bring in every deserving believer into his kingdom as due.

It is highly necessary that every believer and the young in faith particularly learn to feed on the word of Truth for it is the bread of life. The believer feeds on the bread as he learns and obeys the word of God through the teachings of Christ Jesus. It is the bread of life eaten faithfully that turns into the meat of the spirit. The latter may be viewed as the essence or substance of the Divine. It is the essence which remakes the faithful believer over time in the likeness of Christ. It is spiritual meat that constitutes the faith of the believer and gives him reason for hope. It is the meat that brings the dead inner man back to life and sustains the awakened spirit to full maturity in Christ. It takes an adequate measure of the meat of the spirit to anchor the soul in Christ. The soul governs mankind's desires and is an external expression of the spirit within him. The soul is fully nourished when mankind abounds in spiritual meat but famished when such is lacking.

The nourished soul being borne of feeding and living in obedience to the word of Truth is given to seek after the enduring and fulfilling. The nourished soul is not wanton but desires only the good and perfect divinely availed to mankind. Such a soul is ever content for God always hears his petitions and prayers. But the famished soul belongs to him who has not fed on the word of God dutifully or obeyed faithfully as he should have. Such is never content for he harbors an emptiness that can only be divinely filled. Sadly, the famished soul has made no room for God and so cannot have that which he lacks and sorely needs. He is bereft of the spiritual essence which connects man to God and so cannot receive that divinely availed.

The right hand is the icon of Truth and symbolizes that by which mankind reaches out to God whereas the left hand symbolizes that by which he reaches out to the world. The right hand is that by which the faithful receives the life giving and fulfilling good gifts from above. It is also that with which to put up resistance to the enemy. In a spiritual sense therefore, when mankind rejects Truth his right hand will wither and he will be left with the left hand. Where the right hand has withered, mankind can only have those things which will not bring fulfillment. These are the things which entrap mankind into a cycle of wants and purges. When the right hand is withered, wantonness will come to define man's earthly existence If not rescued by the healing power of Christ. The soul entrapped in wantonness has entered a spiritual downward spiral inside a bottomless pit. He has unwittingly become a maggot that lives in unceasing consumption while in an endless hunger. In effect, he has been led away into a barren land.

The famished soul can be revived by the bread of life and the living water of Truth through Christ. Once the soul is revived the spirit within will come back to life. It will be sustained to grow to full maturity if the believer continues in faithful obedience to God's words. The spirit that is immature is of limited service to God but the fully matured in Christ can be of glorious service. Only the fully matured in Christ can produce good and lasting fruits worthy of note. Only the fully matured in Christ can produce works that truly shine before men and serve to draw them to God. Many who profess to follow the way of Christ Jesus are not all true confessors. They are content with putting up the appearance of keeping fellowship with Christ but are unwilling to complete the process of being remade in his full likeness. For such the journey to maturity in Christ through the cross seems too long and much arduous.

The cross that each believer must bear in seeking after Christ is considered to be a mountainous problem and too heavy by many. They deem its humiliation too repulsive to endure and its taste too bitter to stomach. Only those who truly love God and Truth will carry the obligatory cross of Christ to the end. Where there is true love for God, the yoke of Christ does become easy. In truth, the way of the cross leads outside the gate of the city. It leads the believer out of his comfort zone and the 'security' of the props by which the world esteems him. He that seeks to meet up and be remade in the likeness of Christ may lose

Great Vision and Strong Faith

his place in the world. The cross itself stands on a hill so that all will see and mock the seeker after Christ. But such must endure his 'crucifixion' so that his flesh can get out of the way of his spirit. He must be willing to sacrifice the flesh so that his spirit can ascend in divine light. It is the ultimate declaration of faith when man is willing to stand and suffer humiliation for love of Truth. Furthermore, it is the ultimate declaration of love when the unjustly crucified can ask for forgiveness for his detractors.

The faithful that has been rejected and crucified on account of Truth may be given up as dead and done by the faithless. But the latter fail to realize that the cross is a sacred crucible that affords mankind the means of ascension to join up with the Divine in Spirit. False accusation, bearing false witness and condemnation to death is the worst that mankind can do to his fellow. Yet it is by the upending of justice symbolized by the cross that the faithful ascend in spirit to join the ranks of divinity.

He that is joined with God in spirit can afford divine mercy and forgiveness for those that plead through him. The faithful who willingly but unjustly endures crucifixion at the hands of the worldly and yet finds love from within to forgive all will enter into a covenant with the heavenly Father. God will love him without bounds and without end for such measureless and selfless love. Divine blessings will follow such all his days for demonstrating love for God and fellow man beyond all doubt. God uses those that are in covenant with him to give to men in blessing as well as to withhold favors in judgment. All in covenant in this light dwell within the ageless rock where a cleft has been hewn for them with the hammer of faith and chisel of love.

To be in covenant with the Divine is to be remade in the likeness of Christ and given to be victorious in the battle of light against darkness. It is to be remade to be a crusader for God through the light of Christ. The cross endured in the way through Christ guarantees victory in the battle against evil and darkness. To be remade like Christ is to be a shepherd who must defend the flock against the wiles and traps of the prince of darkness of this world. It is to fight not for self or gain but for the greater flock of humanity. The crusader is a useful witness used by God to speak to the hearts of men so as to rescue both individuals as well as the collective soul of humanity.

The faithful are remade in the image of Christ under mercy in order to serve God's purposes and not for personal gain. And so, they are ever obedient to the heavenly Father's will and are his representatives on earth. By unjustly stringing up the innocent on the cross, the people unwittingly elect the unjustly crucified to be the receivers and custodians of the power to heal them. They unwittingly elect such as the ones to show them the way of escape from the grip of darkness and to find the path where redemption in the light of Christ and salvation in eternity with the heavenly Father can be realized.

In as much as every man has an individual besetting sin, so also does every community have a sin that besets its' collective soul. Redemption for each community and its members often comes about through those unjustly crucified by them on account of Truth. Such duly become remade in divine image so that by them any that hunger for righteousness can find new life. Within every community are to be found those divinely elected and remade to be the fountain of living water from whence those souls that thirst for life therein will be filled. Each one so remade is like divine light that arises so that the people can see in Truth to be healed. He that brings such light is given to be perceived so that nothing important will be hidden from him. He will perceive those that desire and sincerely seek after true light but are famished in spirit. It is the latter that he must guide into the knowledge of God. In that vein, he must mercifully forgive any injuries and injustices that he receives from the people as he tries to share the true. He must remain compassionate towards all and mercifully forgive so that light can fully abound for the spiritually blind to finally see.

He that is elected in this light is a son of mercy who must not repay evil for evil. He is called rather to repay evil with goodness. Every elect one is often misused and abused by ungrateful men who mistake grace as graft, kindness for foolishness and meekness for weakness. Every elect one is often exploited by many who will neither acknowledge nor thank him as due. But through it all, duty calls him to take the high road on which only the noble in spirit are found. He must remain on that road for it leads to eternal life and reunion with the Father in divine company. He need not worry for grace is sufficient to sustain him and mercy will meet all his needs along the way. God's promise never to leave or forsake his own has been etched in divine blood for him. And so, he must do the work ordained for him while there is daylight for thereby will God glorify him.

The elect may be in the world but he is no longer of it for he is on his way to a continuing city. Although he stands on earth yet his spirit soars upwards so that his mind touches the sky. The faithful whose spirit soars to the exalted heights will be availed precious seeds from the Divine. But he must return to earth to sow that which he receives for the benefit of humanity. The true seeker does not count costs in his love for God and in following after Christ. He knows that it is the only way to lay up treasures in a place safe from thieves and robbers. He invests all on account of love for God so that he can have contentment of soul now and life everlasting as due reward in the beyond. It is this choice that affords mankind the true and tried gold of God's enduring gifts over the transient that the world offers. All who choose wisely in this light after Christ prove to be worthy vessels good for divine service. Every such vessel must remain ready always to serve the heavenly Father whenever the spirit calls and love urges.

There is good reason why God protects every elect one through the folly of youth and years of spiritual immaturity until maturity to stand before him under mercy. Before any elect one comes to spiritual maturity to then have better knowledge about God's ways, he would be presented with occasions to show mercy and give to others in love. He will give in different and countless ways. He gives because God has put a compassionate and caring heart in everyone destined for divine election from birth. God calls every elect from birth to be compassionate for he has made them to be vessels of mercy. Therefore they cannot help but be merciful and give in love as needed. But they often fail to make the desired impact for they attempt to do the work ordained for the elect but without Christ fully matured within.

It is when Christ comes to full maturity within that the elect learns to use the disposition for compassion to serve God. It is only then that the elect becomes a receiver of everlasting gifts to be shared with other men in the light of Christ. It is only then that he will begin to be used for glorious service. Good intentions alone will not cut the divine cake. The compassionate soul does not fully understand so until the later years of spiritual when he comes into better knowledge of God. Christ is God's guiding light in a dark world that mankind everywhere can freely afford. He can be had for nothing except faith in the goodness of God and by faithful obedience to Truth. Without Christ man labors for self and for nothing but with Christ he labors for God and for life.

As the seeker destined for election grows in faith, his life will begin to be fully reflected through the words of Truth. He will begin to know and see all things through the spirit within. The certainty of his identity in Christ is soon crystallized through experiences with people, places and events in his life. Only then will he realize that through an unquestioned love for God he has become a vessel of compassion and mercy in the mold of Christ. God is the one who molds mankind into either vessels of mercy or wrath. Mercy is man's redeeming love towards another but wrath is his destructive anger towards others. The vessel of mercy is a selfless creation through Christ that abounds in divine attributes within whom the flesh with its wantonness has yielded to the spirit to become of little consequence. To be a vessel of mercy is a manifestation of God's love and spiritual affirmation of the faithful.

Chapter Highlights

- ✓ God goes to great length to bring in the deserving and worthy believer into his kingdom of light.
- ✓ It takes the meat of the spirit to remake the faithful believer over time into the likeness of Christ.
- ✓ The faithless is unwittingly trapped in wantonness as a maggot that lives for unceasing consumption.
- ✓ The famished soul can be nourished to full contentment with bread and living water of truth.
- ✓ It takes true love to suffer unjustly at the hands of sinful men and yet be willing to forgive.
- ✓ To suffer on account of love for God at the hands of the faithless brings man into a divine covenant.
- ✓ The high road on which the noble in spirit are found is the way that leads to eternal life with God.
- ✓ The faithless take grace for graft, kindness for foolishness and meekness for weakness.
- ✓ The faithful soar in spirit to receive divine seeds from above to plant for the benefit of mankind.
- ✓ The believer with a compassionate and caring heart will always be protected through divine love.
- ✓ The vessel of mercy is a selfless creation with the ego mortified so the spirit can fully abound.

Greater love never counts the cost

But remains willing to suffer much

With grace and without complaint

In goodness that makes life bloom

Chapter 15

UNDER DIVINE SUNSHINE

Every elect one dwells under divine mercy and has hitched on an endless celestial ride where the spirit never sleeps. Such is a vessel well prepared to partake of the meat of wisdom from the divine table and to share same in love with those that truly seek in the light of Christ. He is the custodian of divine gifts and a messenger to those willing to receive in true light and good faith. He is one called to walk towards those without wisdom and trust that God will open their hearts to receive the timely needed. He that is used to serve humanity in any noble wise must hold no grievance against those that reject Truth. Rather he must hold out hope for the Spirit of God to induce such that are blind to reach out for redeeming light.

Many who are destined for a place at the heavenly Father's table deny themselves through willful ignorance and disobedience. They know in their hearts that the message of Christ is true for Truth strikes a resonant chord within the soul. The willfully disobedient may not know him as God but everyone realizes that there is an overarching wisdom that pervades through creation. The willful deny themselves the chance to reconnect with the Creator due to pride and fear of rejection by the world. God knows this too well and has an elect one positioned within every community. The elect or the christened in light is one from among the people that God has anointed to be the vessel through which they may learn about him better. Every elect one is anointed to help frame the way into the kingdom of God for all who sincerely seek. Life in the kingdom of God is where darkness has been chased away and divine light shines as the sun within all hearts.

God makes more room within the divine fold for everyone who seeks out the lost in order to share the light of Christ with them. He reveals more to the faithful who labors in light and love through Christ so that others may receive true knowledge. He teaches his way and gives more to him who pours out himself into others in mercy. The divine bowl of mercy serves to refill all the vessels that faithfully empty themselves into others. In that wise, God becomes better known to him who will make others to know the heavenly way better. Everyone who serves faithfully to share the light of Christ will be brought to a place closer to God's heart. He will drink deeper and fuller to the source of all wisdom. He will be an outlet for those certain days in certain places when the power of God will be present to 'attend' to everybody's need in light and love. Such a one must always remain ready to serve as a conduit of hope for others during those certain occasions when the healing waters are stirred up by the divine Father.

There is a season appointed for everyone in which God will be near and at hand for him. That season is limited and must not be wasted. It is much like the 'touch of lightning' offered from Heaven to earth to enlighten as well as heal mankind. It is in those times that the heavenly alights on the earthly. He that has been chosen will sense the divine presence and know that God is at hand. He must not make the mistake of sounding out the opinion of others when he senses the touch or hears the call of the Divine. It may not be the appointed season for those others just yet. He must listen to his heart and answer as Heaven calls him in love. Every man's heart is his best sounding board. Indeed man can be his own best friend if he chooses wisely or worst enemy if he chooses poorly.

The believer that faithfully obeys the call and opens his heart to God will be guided from the shadowy into a greater light of understanding. He that opens up will have the light of Truth shine within and around him to guide him on to the divine path. Like a friend that is true for all times, the light of Truth never grows dim or disappears when the believer remains faithful. But there is always a cross to bear and price to pay to keep the light of Truth aglow. The believer must be willing to bear his cross as called for he will end up in a place far greater than the world holds out. He will be able to ascend in spirit to come into a realm where divine gifts are availed and nothing is wanted. Things will no longer be as in the past when he could not produce good outcomes, for he will be led by the Holy Spirit in all endeavors to do marvelously.

He within whom God's light glows has become part of his everlasting plan for humanity and a building block of his kingdom on earth. He is one who has become prepared as a model to draw others to the kingdom way. He who seeks for a place in the kingdom of God must do so in Truth. It is only by Truth that the seeker can prove worthy of his calling and be a good custodian of that which God entrusts to mankind in love. Divine gifts are not without accountability. There is a season of reckoning and a time of validation when every recipient is graded to determine how well he has performed with what God has entrusted to him. He that is proven worthy will be entrusted with more. But he that has not been diligent but rather indolent will be dispossessed of that which had been entrusted to him. A great lesson that needs to be learned in the kingdom way is that divine gifts abound with diligent use but atrophy with neglect and abuse.

The believer that is faithful and diligent in the use of the gifts availed to him will grow to become a building block of the kingdom of God. Such may seem little to the world but he will be esteemed well by God. He who profanes the gifts will turn out to be an empty shell. He may be held in high esteem by the world but he will have little within him of value to God. Such is one who looks great in appearance and sounds very knowledgeable about spiritual matters but lacks the essence of the divine upon which the kingdom of God is built. Worthiness before God comes from diligent searching and faithful living in accordance with the word of Truth. He that searches diligently and obeys faithfully will begin to grow in the inner man in new life much like an embryo laid in the cocoon of love to be nourished with the essence of Christ. In the fullness of time and in accordance with divine will, he will grow to full maturity in Christ.

It takes full maturity in Christ to be a good and worthy custodian of divine gifts. There is an unmistakable and innocent other-worldliness about the seeker who has grown to spiritual maturity in Christ. It is a glow that shines forth from within. It speaks to the fact that his heart has been lit as a lamp of God to give sight to anyone who cares enough to embrace Truth. It takes a little while for the believer that is matured to understand what he has become through Christ and how to use it to further the kingdom of God. The believer may look the same on the outside but he is totally different within where Christ has grown to full maturity. He that is fully matured in Christ has been imputed with the mind of the Divine. It takes a a while to comprehend its full significance but the truth is that the fully matured in Christ has become a son of God able to know and do much in the spirit of the divine.

The fully matured in Christ has scaled the mountain of faith to come into full light thereby. He has been fitted with spiritual wings and connected with the source of all wisdom from whence the knowledge to change the world for better is availed. The wisdom to know and the power to do belong to God but he that is connected to the Divine will have access to same through Christ. However he must use whatever is availed to him for the benefit and welfare of humanity as the spirit of God leads him.

The matured in Christ are bestowed with strong faith and the vision to see from a heavenly perspective. The works of glory take greater spiritual enlightenment and require faith that perseveres through all odds. All that Christ avails is received freely for the works that bring God due glory. The matured in Christ do not seek to exploit men for gain but to help them join Heaven's eternal feast of love. He who seeks his own gain dishonors both the gift and the giver. He is the unfaithful one and a blight that is not welcome to the divine feast. But he that is faithful to share divine gifts is highly valued by God as the best that man can become through the light and love of Christ.

Chapter Highlights

- ✓ Life in the kingdom of God is an endless ride under the sunshine of love where the spirit never sleeps.
- ✓ New life is where darkness has been chased away so that light can always shine within the heart.
- ✓ God is better known to those who make the way of Christ better known to others.
- ✓ The believer in whose heart the light of God shines has found a trustworthy guide through life.
- ✓ The faithful that are part of God's redeeming plan are able to do works divinely ordained for glory.
- ✓ The only way for mankind to find welcome in God's kingdom is to seek after him in Truth.
- ✓ The faithful believer is remade in likeness of the divine while shielded in the cocoon of love.
- ✓ The believer whose heart has been lit as a lamp of God to give sight to others will glow from within.
- ✓ The heart that has been lit with the flame of love is highly prized by God and treasured in Heaven.
- ✓ The works ordained for glory take greater spiritual enlightenment and require faith that perseveres.
- ✓ The believer that has a true understanding of Truth has a place of honor at the divine feast of Christ.
- ✓ The faithful do come to know and see the grand picture of what good plans God has for mankind.

In faith hope attends as love beckons

As willing sacrifice deep from the soul

It is the gift that opens up a wellspring

From which life's healing stream flows

Chapter 16

MARKS OF THE NEW LIFE

The christened in light is the faithful believer who has been recreated in the image of Christ. Only those who have been remade in this image are able to reconnect in spirit with God the Father. Such were once sinners like all but cared enough and dared to cry out to God in hope for salvation by grace through faith in Christ Jesus. They made the life changing decision to cast aside pride and confess their past sins as well as ask for forgiveness from God in good faith. In faithfulness to his promise of forgiveness for the truly contrite heart, the heavenly Father has forgiven, redeemed and spiritually fitted them for useful service in his kingdom of light. In the course of time and by spiritual transformation, they have become woven into the fabric of the eternal as God's own sons. As such, they have become covered with the golden fleece of the Lamb of sacrifice which protects mortals from the ravages of time. As such they wear the robe of immortality fully and fully abound in new life in Christ with a spirit which has vanquished death.

The golden fleece of the lamb is that which covers God's tabernacles on earth and is afforded through sacrificial love in the light and love of Christ. The tabernacles are the hearts which have become lit with the flame of love through Christ to become God's dwelling place on earth. Such have unrequited love for God and labor to hold up the flame so that those who seek after Truth can see in true light. These tabernacles are the sons through whom God commands his sovereign will on earth. Since God has chosen them as his dwelling place on earth, whoever can perceive his sons has 'seen' God for he has filled them with his divine presence and godly attributes.

It is the most exalted honor when a once debased creature such as mankind is judged to be worthy of divine company. It is cause for great joy when man is judged to be holy and acceptable by God to be woven into the fabric of eternal life. It is an undeniable testament to the longsuffering and forgiving nature of God as well as the ability of strong faith to accomplish mighty works through Christ. It takes such faith to turn a tiny seed into a mighty tree and mere mortals into giants whose minds are in tune with the Divine. Such strong faith is divinely availed, nourished by the word of Truth and takes time to mature.

Strong faith in God can bring the dead and dying back to life. It is only those who possess strong faith that can stand in the congregation of the mighty. Strong faith is such that is wrought through trials by the upright in spirit that fear God. It is faith wrought through the cross as the crucible that breeds immortal souls. It is the faith of those who through no fault of their own endure much suffering and pain at the hands of the worldly on account of their love for Truth. It is faith wrought by suffering for goodness sake in the light of Christ so that mankind the product of the base dust of the earth can be purified into the golden of Heaven. The golden realized is eternal and far outweighs the glory of the earthly left behind.

All who have been crucified and suffered unjustly on account of Christ share a common experience. They understand each other's pains, sacrifices and unrequited love for God. They bear the nail marks of crucifixion and carry deep wounds unjustly on account of love for God and Truth. They have faithfully followed in the footsteps of Christ Jesus to join up with him within the divine fold. Therein they have come to experience love bestowed by God on the beloved that is everlasting and is never severed. Therein the heavenly Father has reserved a place very close to his divine heart for them as due reward for troubles endured in nobility of spirt.

The place close to God's heart is where the veil of Heaven is lifted so that the noble in spirit can become privy to the will of God. God wills and acts through such that are noble for they are ever faithful in serving his purposes on earth.

He avails knowledge and wisdom that is not taught by man but bestowed in light and love from above. And so the noble in spirit come to be custodians of the hidden glimpsed from behind the veil of Heaven as well as extensions of the commanding impulse by which the heavenly order is translated on earth.

Mankind's incomprehensible folly is his penchant to crucify the noble in spirit and strong of faith. But by divine mercy, the deep marks of the nails used to crucify them serve to open up the wellspring of new life in such. Living water, sweet and pure, flows from their hearts to bring life to those willing to embrace Truth. All who bear the nails marks of cannot help but be merciful. Mercy is the currency of exchange for the treasures of Heaven. The goodness and tender mercies of God follow the noble in spirit for they are the compassionate of heart well fitted in Christ. They are ever merciful even as many despitefully use them. It takes mercy to bring mankind to the parkway of life where it is not necessary to rush about but to calmly travel on. The parkway of life is the amazing place of faith-rest where the good and perfect gifts are availed to be realized in the light of Christ. It is life lived in the kingdom of God by those who have been adopted as sons. It is a place not seen with the eyes of the flesh but life that can be experienced through the spirit.

The kingdom of God can be known by the noble in spirit

Marks of the New Life

for it is the field of dreams that only the pure of heart can 'see'. He to whom the kingdom of God is revealed is also availed perception of spirit so that the needful things will be made plain and noting can be hidden from him. He will no longer walk about blindly on earth as he did in times past and as many still do. Because all is done in accordance with God's will in his kingdom, those who can 'see' in spirit to enter therein are given to have fruitful outcomes in their labors. The earthly endeavors of such that dwell therein shine before men as the Divine acts through them to bring about fulfilling and enduring outcomes.

The believer that gains a place in the kingdom of God has entered a precious realm. Life in the kingdom of God triggers an overwhelming desire in the believer to share the reality of what is possible through Christ so others can experience the same. They that dwell in the kingdom of God are willingly to sacrifice everything and hold nothing back. Sadly most men are dismissive of that which is offered in light through Christ and miss out on the chance to experience the Divine. But for those who heed Truth, the knowledge and experience become real as they are guided in true light to mature in Christ through grace to stand before God under mercy.

He that is matured in the spirit of Christ to stand under divine mercy has passed judgment in true light and will be an elect one changed into the likeness of the Divine. As a result, he will be bestowed with the divine mind as a spiritual clone of Christ Jesus. He will also become the sacrificial lamb for those who will believe and follow after him in the light of Christ. Anyone who heeds him and follows through in good faith will be well guided to abound in Christ in accordance with God's will. Every elect one has been chosen to make sacrifices and receive gifts from God on behalf of others. Thereby he saves the trip up the mountain for those who desire Truth but lack the strong faith needed to climb to faith's summit. Every elect one is a sacrificial lamb wholly acceptable to God and is a representative model elected for those that hunger after righteousness but have not yet realized strong faith.

There is an elect one anointed by God to attend every true seeker. The elect is revealed to the seeker when he sets his heart after God in humility and true penitence. God has earmarked the elect from the foundation of time. More often than not, their own will reject and crucify them for being such strange 'characters' in their midst. It is this rejection at the hands of the people which every elect must pass that defines the heart of the cross. But yet, it is the willingness to pass through the heart of the cross which defines the essence of Christ and comes to mark the elect as sons of light. The sons are given to rule together in the kingdom of God as one in the spirit of Christ as the noble of soul and pure in spirit who can be trusted to serve on behalf of the people in true light.

The elect are true messengers who readily answer God's call to go on behalf of others. And so they ascend and descend in spirit on the celestial stairway to offer up petitions and bring down answers. They are the vessels well-prepared to receive that which speaks to the here and now. They receive due and prescient knowledge from the throne of the heavenly Father as needed and made possible by the Holy Ghost. Even though the elect receive privileged information not availed to all yet they share such knowledge with all who embrace Truth in good faith. In truth, Heaven's gift to mankind is obtained in love to be shared with the beloved flock in the light of Christ.

Faithfulness in the light of Christ costs the elect much in the world but God's promise is to restore that lost after his kingdom been sought and realized. Every elect one stands to gain back all which appears to be seemingly lost in the way after Christ. Each has to be worthy of the investiture on him by the Father as a son of light. Every elect one is deemed an elder in faith who knows the way and is called upon to point it out to the young in faith who do not yet know. He is called to model Christ for those who seek but have yet to find true light. Each elect brings nothing of the self in this call save a heart that loves God. It is on that account that Providence attends in the way to meet their daily needs through Christ. The elect have joined the ranks of the exalted that have nothing but yet have everything and know nothing but know everything through Christ. All who have joined this elect body not only share and receive everything in grace but are duly refilled with needed provisions by the heavenly Father in mercy.

Every seeker must be ready to bear a nail mark in his body so that the old nature can remain dead and new life may abound. Life in Christ is about sacrifices made in love by some so that others can come into light of the Divine. Christ leads from the darkness of the world into the starry and marvelous light of God. The fluffy and wasteful wants of the world preclude the spirit from soaring to reach the light and starry. The worldly is weighty and has to be pruned from mankind before his spirit can intermeddle with the Divine. With Christ, mankind is able to leave the old self behind and to have it replaced with a new reborn in light. The reborn is a more streamlined new self that is much better and quicker in spirit. The new creature in Christ is freed from the world's bondage and is able to soar up to the heavenly heights where the exalted in spirit gather. The exalted in spirit live to serve God's will under mercy. He that soars heavenly in spirit can ask of God to receive that which his heart desires but he must also be willing to do all that the Father asks of him. And so, his lot in life is to buckle down in strong faith for the never ending ride of amazement between Heaven and earth.

Chapter Highlights

- ✓ The believer covered with the fleece of the Lamb of sacrifice has been woven into the fabric of life.
- ✓ The sons of God are his tabernacles on earth and are bestowed with immortality of soul.
- ✓ It is through suffering on account of goodness that base man is purified into a son of Heaven.
- ✓ Strong faith in God regardless of circumstance is the breeding ground of immortal souls.
- ✓ Those that truly bear the cross of Christ understand each other's pains, sacrifices and love for Truth.
- ✓ The deep marks of the nails used to crucify the faithful open up a wellspring of new life.
- ✓ The parkway of life is the place of the amazing and those that travel thereon have come into faith rest.
- ✓ The kingdom of God is the field of dreams that only the pure of heart can perceive.
- ✓ The faithful make willing sacrifices so others can come to know God and find contentment of soul.
- ✓ The elect are the noble of soul and saintly in spirit who can be trusted by God to serve him faithfully.
- ✓ Every believer must be ready to bear the nail marks of Christ so that the old nature can remain dead.
- ✓ The heavenly way is about sacrifices made in love so that many can come to experience the Divine.

Certainty makes for simplicity and orderliness

But variance does breed complications in life

Heaven's blessings alight not on the uncertain

Neither will hope attend in strife or confusion

Chapter 17

PEACE FOR THE CERTAIN

The believer who is spiritually reconciled with God will subsequently be at peace within and with all things in creation. He will begin to hear the inaudible whispers that come from all that surrounds him. The ear of the spirit within him will be tuned to pick up much of what everything around him is communicating. He will realize that he has become a wireless receiver that walks about in a sea of information that most men are not aware of. Because he is spiritually in tune with the Creator and creation, he is given to walk on the path of righteousness for only those who are can do so. As a result, he will no longer cast about blindly wherever, whenever and however in life for he can see in true light to be sure of where he is going. He will in effect begin to live a focused and purposed life suited to produce outcomes that delight the heart as well as please the heavenly Father.

He who walks on the path of righteousness will cease from cutting corners and looking for short cuts in his earthly endeavors. He will come to fully understand that there is a right way and appointed seasons to do things. He will catch the spirit that leads mankind to make the path straight, lay the foundation square and build things the right way. Such is the spirit that attends full maturity in Christ and embodies the divine wind of change that heralds the everlasting. Full maturity in the spirit of Christ is the issuing forth of God's blessed anointing and the projection of divine light on the faithful seeker. The wind of change that heralds full maturity in Christ is often a stormy whirlwind that sweeps away the old to reset things in new light for the seeker. The stormy wind is the hammerhead for breaking up the hard and stony ground so that it may be won over for God. The soil is prepared well before Christ arrives to plant the divine precious seeds, the candle stand is positioned before the candle is lit and the lesser is laid out before the greater is tendered.

It is of no use to learn all the words of scripture but miss the spirit of new life in Christ embodied within the words. He who knows and can quote all of scripture but lacks the divine anointing of the spirit within those words has nothing. He will never be able to fulfill the spirit of the law though he may quote and spout them. He who has the spirit of Truth may not know all that is written about God's laws but he will be divinely guided to fulfill them. There is an underlying truth and a common thread that runs through the scriptures that is difficult for many to 'see'. It is difficult because they lack the faith to trust God who they cannot see. They lack the wisdom and spiritual guidance to fathom words that are often divinely cloaked in the purest of light. The words of scriptures are really about the Spirit of God presenting the same Truth in 'diverse manners and sundry times' to mankind that is hard of hearing in the hope that it will get through at the appointed time for him to comprehend in better light.

The heavenly Father will bend down and do all he can to meet man at his lowly intransigent level. He who knows a little scripture and lives by that is far better than he who knows a lot but will not live by what he knows. The former is a faithful believer but the latter is a noisy drum that is filled with empty words. His words though plentiful and enthralling will lack the power of divine anointing. He that is filled with such empty words has fallen into the sin of the scribes and Pharisees. The door that leads to the Father eludes such but yet they refuse to allow those that know to show the way. The believer who writes the words of scripture in the tablet of his heart and lives accordingly will be instructed into the hidden truths and mysteries. He will lay up a priceless treasure in his heart from which will spring forth things that are new but old. He will duly become privy to the unspoken things of God understood only as the Holy Ghost speaks to the faithful heart.

The scriptures cease to be just words when the faithful

become privy to the hidden truths. Only then do the words coalesce into pictures which show up repeatedly all over. Colors and shades within the pictures may differ but the contents remain the same. It is God using certain people in certain ways to highlight and contrast the two ways of life on earth. One is the way of Christ which leads to life and the other is the way of the world that leads to death. The characters may differ but the underlying truth and outcome remain the same. The encompassing message is that man does not stand a chance against evil by himself. He needs divine intervention to help him and he can have it through Christ. Christ Jesus is the way of escape that God has set aside so mankind can overcome the prince of the darkness of this world. He that trusts in the faithful promise that God has made through Christ will grow in spirit to 'see' the pictures in the scriptures. As he lives in faithful obedience to that seen, he will grow from glimpsing the pictures to fully comprehend the harmony and timeless treasure within the whole of God's truth.

The faithful that gets the picture and understands the harmony within the scriptures has become an eater of the fruit of the fig tree. The words of scripture are mostly figurative but yet true and fulfilling. This is the mystery and the genius of God's divine mind. The fig tree is the tree of life whose fruit can only be afforded by those who have attained a certain level of spiritual maturity. He who eats and digests the fruit of the fig tree will be in communion with the Divine. God communicates in pictures for it is a universal medium that needs no translation. It is indeed true that one picture is better than a thousand words. It is also true that one who is in communal fellowship with God can chase a thousand that are faithless. Language is a local medium that divides and separates mankind. It muddles and limits communion of spirit among humanity. It was instituted at Babel in order to throw man for a loop. It is a way for the heavenly Father to instruct mankind that there are such things that cannot be accomplished by human strength or power but in the spirit of the living God. It is a way for God to let mankind know that he only determines who is spiritually worthy regardless of what each man thinks of self. It is a preventive measure to preclude mankind from taking the base things of the earth to Heaven. It is God's way to tell all that mankind must first be purified in spirit by living in obedience to the words of Truth before he can afford to ascend to the starry heights to then bring the heavenly down to earth.

The faithful believer who can ascend to the heavenly heights is able to see the true picture of the world that God sees. He will no longer be deceived by the worldly for his eyes can 'see' from the mountain top. He has ascended to the summit of the mount where mankind is transfigured and soaked in the pure mist of true understanding. The transfigured is a living tabernacle not planted in one place but able to go in spirit as the Father sends him. Such is given to communicate less with words but more in pictures and actions. The medium of pictures is the language of light and truth. A picture leaves a true impression on the mind that tells no lies. It is the most faithful and effective medium to teach the mind, feed the soul and nourish man's spirit. The words of scripture paint one grand picture of his glorious family as God instructs mankind about outcomes, fruits, works and end results. God speaks not about persons but about his family. There comes a season in the life of every faithful believer when he begins to see himself and his place within that family. When that comes about, he will become the selfless in spirit who has entered the season of restoration where goodness and mercy readily come to attend him in life.

Simply put, restoration is the process of bringing things back to how they should be or putting contents back into the empty. It is the means by which things are re-created or new things are brought out from the old. Restoration emanates from the hub of creation which is at the heart of God. It is from thence that the power to rebuild broken down things and to bring dead things back to life issue forth. There is usually a set of problems that appear mountainous and insurmountable to the believer at the commencement of restoration. It takes divine wisdom bestowed from the heavenly Father to afford the believer the means to break down the mountainous that confronts him. Only then will he discover that within the mountain in the way are the seeds that God will use to glorify him.

The seeds of glory are already there but are found as gold dust sprinkled in the stream of living water that flows within the mountain in the way. The seeds of glory are found within that which had seemed to block the way. But first the seeker must be shown the way into the heart of the mountain. A way has to be made for him where hitherto none had seemed to be. A cleft has to be made for him in the Rock. The eye of the inner man has to be opened so that he can see that which has always been there but not perceived. The seeker could not see before because his spirit had been cast down by the heavy cross that he had to carry. He did not realize then that the burden of the cross will free the spirit within him to see in greater light. Only the free in spirit can afford the coin that is the toll to Providence. The coin affords the donkey that the seeker rides in his 'Hosanna' parade so he can enter into the peace that passes understanding. The donkey is that vehicle which has been prepositioned and tethered for the seeker. The vehicle is there but it can only be seen in the true and pure humble light of Christ. It is the vehicle by which the faithful come into Providence and under the mercy of God. And so by divine mercy the faithful in Christ come to be justified and shown a way out of troubles.

The process of restoration begins with full immersion in Truth but concludes with baptism in the fire of the spirit of

Christ. Immersion in Truth or the baptism of John serves to keep the spiritual walk of the believer simple, orderly and purposed. Simplicity, orderliness and purpose lead to certainty. Complexity, disorderliness and variance lead to uncertainty. God does not restore the uncertain or bless the confused. The shell of the mountain in the way of restoration protects the valuable seeds hidden within its heart. The seeds are capsules of the glorious that have been touched by the hand of the Divine and watered by the purified mists of Truth. Once planted, the seeds of glory will sprout to kiss the heavens and branch out to touch the horizons so that all men can see what the hand of the Lord has done. And so the mountain that confronts the faithful in the way always breaks out in joyful song to induce mankind to praise God for his marvelous doings.

The faithful believer that has been entrusted with seeds of the glorious must be diligent to plant them for such are precious. The seeds of glory are framed in great vision. Great vision takes strong faith to be made manifest so all can see what God has done. The trustee of the seed must put the 'spirit' of discouragement behind so that he can embrace the spirit of power and a sound mind. This can only happen when he connects to the Holy Spirit through Christ. The Holy Spirit is the enabler of the faithful. The heavenly Father will not deny the request of the trustee of his priceless seeds. He who carries the priceless seeds is God's chosen vessel to be used for glory. God hides the seeds of glory in hearts where the enemy cannot touch such. Every trustee of the seed is also shielded from the corruption of worldliness so that he can remain prepared to be the good steward in the season of restoration.

God confides in the chosen in order to avail knowledge that is hidden from others. In this season of information overload, true wealth is knowledge that is not commonly available. Knowledge and wisdom from the divine Father is given freely but it is not free. It is not to be misused or abused but used for glorious service in God's name through Christ. The fullness of the riches in the divine treasure chest is limitless. The custodian of the priceless must remove himself from doubters and anything else that will distract him from the purpose ordained for him. He must plant so that he can have abundant harvest as due. Abundance is his due reward for faithfulness and love for God. Such is the harvest that awaits the good custodian who faithfully plants as God instructs and the spirit leads.

The faithful believer that has come into restoration has intermeddled with and been grafted into the source of all wisdom. He must remain there with Christ at the center of his life so that he can continue in victorious living. He must continue to walk in the light of Christ so as to be assured of abundant harvest for his labors. He must the divine command that all pass through the door of Christ always in order to find both spiritual and earthly nourishment. The blood of the Lamb of sacrifice must be on the doorposts of his heart to serve and protect him in his going out and coming in. He that is in restoration has died and is resurrected with Christ. He has become the selfless with a new name and new life that no longer lives for self but for all. It is for such in restoration that God has promised never to leave or forsake. This is victory promised, victory hoped for and victory attained. It is life triumphant realized through Christ. The custodian of the precious seed must not seek after the praise of men for such praise perverts the gift and infects the seed. He must remain in the wings and let God take center stage so as to remain justified in all his ways. He must protect the divine seeds in the treasure chest of his heart with diligent love so that he may continue to bring out things that are new but old.

The believer can only protect the precious by immersion and obedience to Truth in the light of Christ. Obedience to truth offers the believer a chance to clean up his spiritual life. It affords the faithful a means to shake off the world and have a chance to be sprinkled with the dust of eternity. Truth eliminates areas of spiritual weakness in the life of the believer that may expose him to attack and possible defeat by the forces of darkness. Immersion in Truth is the rinsing off of the residual mud cake of the world so that the faithful can be primed for the eternal. It is the final preparation before the faithful believer who has been seeking after him can finally meet up with Christ.

Immersion in Truth serves to disengage the halting and hindering in the life of the seeker so that he can never be left behind again once he has met up with Christ. Immersion in Truth or baptism of John can be likened to Moses leading the Hebrews of old to the doorsteps of the new land wherein he cannot enter. It is the transition from the highest of the less into the lowest of the greater. It is being called up from the minor to the major league of faith. Baptism in Truth changes and resets the perspective of the believer permanently from the earthly to the heavenly. It helps him to keep his eyes fixed and his heart tuned to God. It serves to remind the seeker why he is here, what he should be doing with his time, how he should be doing it and who he should be doing it for. Full immersion or baptism in Truth is the last cleansing of the mind before the faithful is ushered into the order of Christ.

The faithful believer that has met up to be ushered into the order of Christ will seem to be alone but he is not for he has entered into a select company. He is connected in spirit to an unseen innumerable host with Christ Jesus leading the way. There will be times when he may appear to be that lone voice in a wilderness filled with the deaf and blind determined to go their own way but going nowhere really. It is in such times that he may weary, worry and wonder if he has labored in vain and for naught. But he must persevere in nurturing the seed of Truth entrusted to him for such never fails to bear fruit in due season. God's work may be stymied for a while but it is never stopped as long as it is accompanied by strong faith and great vision.

There is a cycle of the feeling of emptiness followed by that of revival that accompanies work in the kingdom of God. And so the laborer for God needs to be spiritually refilled in between so that he may in turn fill others in a repetitive cycle. It is like recharging a battery depleted after usage for the next duty cycle. It is the vessel being empowered by the Master to be used for works of glory. The believer not used in this stead will have nothing to show for his faith for the validation and utility value of the vessel lies in its usage to do work pleasing to God. The chosen may appear little in the eyes of the world and be marginalized to the fringes of society yet he occupies an exalted place in the universal scheme of things. He will grow from the 'little one' to stand up in the congregation of the mighty before God and bask in the glory of faithful service to the Divine.

Chapter Highlights

- ✓ It takes reconciliation with God for man to find peace within and with all things in creation.
- ✓ He that quotes the words of scripture but lacks the spirit therein in him has nothing before God.
- ✓ The underlying reason for God's gift of Christ is that man does not stand a chance against evil alone.
- ✓ The mystery of God's sacred truths is that such are figurative yet true and ever fulfilled.
- ✓ The fully matured in spirit can ascend to the exalted realm to perceive the world as God does.
- ✓ The seeds of glory lie within faith-mountain as sprinkles of golden dust in a stream of living water.
- ✓ Only God can avail mankind the seed of glory that sprouts from earth to heaven when planted.
- ✓ God hides the seed of glory in the heart of the faithful believer where the enemy cannot touch it.
- ✓ Obedience to Truth removes the hindering so the seeker never falls behind once joined with Christ.
- ✓ The works of glory may be stymied for a while by the enemy but such are never stopped.

Humanity's true face can be seen in love

Where the enduring and fulfilling abound

In a place where meekness rules the heart

And in a time to seek redress not impress

Chapter 18

LIGHT IN A DARK SEA

The heavenly heights offer a unique perspective from which to view life on earth in a true and pure light. Seen from above, the earth is a sea of darkness interspersed with points of light. The points of light are those whose souls have been washed by the words of Truth and whose hearts have been lit as altars to serve God and humanity in love. The darkness that surrounds the points of light is the pervasive evil found within the hearts of many in the world. However God's eyes are forever fixed on the points of light in doting love to protect them from the evil wind of the worldly that surrounds them.

Every heart lit with the flame of love is so much treasured by God that his ear is always ready to hear their prayers. It is on account of such high regard for them, which must not be overlooked, that God is very much concerned with protecting them from the darkness and evil that surrounds them in the world. It is for such whose hearts have been lit as candles that the bowls of goodness and tender mercies are laid out. Heaven's offerings to mankind can be thought of as bowls filled with life's good gifts as well as acts of goodness and mercy tendered in love. The contents of the bowls are there to delight the hearts lit aflame with love as it pleases the heavenly Father for they are joined with him in spirit through Christ. Such hearts are tabernacles for the spirit of God to dwell and also vessels through which mercy is poured out on earth.

Every heart aflame with love has been prepared to serve as a vessel of mercy on earth with the light of Christ as life's guide. Such vessels often suffer much adversity in the world for love of God and devotion to Christ. Yet they remain willingly to endure and persevere after Christ to the end. Rejection and undeserved hatred by the world on account of love for God and Truth never deter the truly faithful. They refuse to cast blame but choose rather to ask for God's forgiveness for the ignorance of men. The willingness to bear the shame and loneliness of the cross in grace serves to validate the faithful before God. Such grace commends the faithful in Christ well to make communion between the heavenly and earthly possible. He that can commune in that light has become a hybrid of two worlds that can go for other men where they are not able to go. He can listen in on things that other men are not able to hear and share knowledge garnered thereby. In effect, he has joined in the divinely ordained mission to bring wisdom from heavenly to earthly places in the light of Christ to help remake earth in the order of Heaven.

The curse of Babel is reversed for him that has been divinely appointed to help remake earth in the order of Heaven. He will be divinely availed the universal language of Truth whereby all in creation will understand him and he will understand them in spirit. The wall of division that separates mankind will be broken down for him so that he will come to dwell in spirit where all feed together in peace. He will be given to speak in figures and frame pictures with words. The pictures that he frames with his words have been glimpsed with the eye of the inner man. Such pictures reflect Truth by which God's divine will is manifested. God's will is forward looking and leads to the future. The ultimate will of God is regeneration for his creation. He that is privy to divine will is also availed the means to revitalize necessary things in life. He will be led in spirit to do the right thing at the right time as one who has come into the season of regeneration. However such must proceed with due diligence and use that availed to get God's business duly done with his time on earth.

It costs the believer his place in the world and many of the wanted things in life before he can come into the season of regeneration. The latter is found under mercy by those that wisely sought after the kingdom of God first. He that has come into the season of regeneration has a confidence which pervades his nature and governs everything that he says and does. It is this other-worldly confidence that communicates that Christ has come to full maturity within the believer and that which attracts many to Truth.

The gift of Christ fully matured and arisen in the believer must be used to serve humanity and bring God due glory. The matured in Christ must be ready at all times to bear testimony to others about the confidence that frames his life. It is confidence borne of unrequited love, unbreakable promises and the blessings of the heavenly Father which has come to attend his life. The spirit of fear departs to be replaced by that of power and a sharp mind when Christ matures and is arisen within the believer. He that is bestowed with such power and a sharp mind must remain faithful always to serve God's will in true light.

Christ knows what the future will look like for mankind. He knows what will be needful in the future and what will not be. It all works together under God's provident will to yield the enduring and fulfilling for the faithful believer. It is life divinely appointed in the light of Christ for those that dwell under the mercy of God. In order to be worthy to be called therein, the believer must remain a clean vessel, holy and acceptable to be used by God. Surely the earth is his creation but the heavenly Father needs the faithful who understand his way to help manage things the right way.

There is a mass of men and women all over the world that

love and follow in light after Christ to God's approval. They have followed in good faith to meet up with Christ in that place close to the heart of God. Such are perfect before God as mankind can be but continuously garnering the attributes of the divine in an unending everlasting process. They are the beloved of God held in the protective palm of his hand as one carefully holds the precious pearl. The stars of the night sky are emblematic of them. Each star occupies the place ordained for it from the beginning of time to help spell out God's plan and intention for the perceptive eye to see. In the same wise, the faithful are led to occupy the earthly lots that the Father has ordained for them as starry spirits to shine thereabouts in reflection of his divine will. In the fullness of time, as they complete their earthly round, these starry spirits do return to their heavenly abode as the chosen given to twinkle in love and life everlasting within the Divine fold.

God's plan and intentions are there for the perceptive in spirit to see in the night sky. The writings in the night sky can only be read by the chosen that have been bestowed with the eye to do so. The latter are the matured in Christ that are privy to the divine will. Such have passed judgment in God's eye so that nothing is hidden from them. The writings spell out divine edicts that are there for everyone to see for the sky is a universal canvas. Sadly most men are spiritually blind and not aware that the writings are there. Others are sight impaired and know that the writings are there but are unable to read them. However a select few can see and read them. These are the bearers of his divine light who have been chosen for eternal life with the heavenly Father. Such pass through the world and leave a trail of enlightenment everywhere during their brief sojourn on earth. They leave handiworks that shine before men and are showcases for God's endowments on mankind to be fully displayed. Those who follow them will never go wrong for they are vehicles used to carry out the divine sovereign will on earth.

The matured in Christ have been nurtured in the cocoon of love under divine mercy as the seedlings of the unfolding re-creation of the earth. They are the embryos that will be transplanted to populate the new that looms on the horizon. These worthy souls are the link between the passing world and the emerging one. As the current age passes away because it is appointed for all earthly things to die, another will emerge as the new Heaven on earth. The faithful and worthy before God comprise the nursery for the new earth to come. They are enmeshed in a perfecting process within the cocoon of God's love to be transformed therein into the divine image. Such are then used to induce those that interact with them on earth into a spiritual awakening in the light of Christ.

The whole of creation is waiting for noble in spirit bred in the cocoon of love under mercy and changed into a divine image to show in full force. Their experience in the cocoon of love translates into the pattern for victorious living that will be manifested in the new age of the earth to come. Their time and experience in the cocoon of God's love has prepared them in spirit with the knowledge needed to master the future. And so, they have become the visionaries and guiding lights appointed to lead mankind into a better future. Without consciously being aware of it, such are living at the present time as mankind will come to live in the future that awaits humanity. As this age comes to its inevitable end, there will be a cosmic silence or turning around point when things will change to trend upwards to the good and perfect.

The season of the good and perfect is that which creation is waiting for. It is the season that heralds the glorious dawn of humanity. It is the dawn of the day of the new man in Christ purified of heart and noble in spirit. It is the age for those who have chosen the fruit of the tree of life through Christ. Such have chosen the wisdom of God over the fruit of the knowledge of good and evil which stokes the darkness in the world. All who choose wisdom will no longer settle for less and exhaust precious time to seek an impossible balance between good and evil. Rather they will break free from evil to finally attain the good and perfect which has always been the heavenly Father's wish for mankind from the beginning of creation. All who are appointed to see the dawn of the good and perfect are duly woven into the fabric of life. All who are woven therein have realized the everlasting from which there is no separation for it is death swallowed up in victory by life.

All who have been chosen for the new age are also bestowed with a life inducing spirit. The things that their embrace will thrive to endure and those things that they reject will not. As couriers of the divine spark in this wise, they embody seeds of new life that bring about a quickening and re-awakening of spirit in the lifeless. That which bring is light that thaws out the wintry in the dormant spirit in order to usher in the spring of new life.

The flesh is the great inhibitor of man's spirit but he needs it for the time of his brief existence on earth. The flesh always wars against the spirit to make man susceptible to the corruption in the world. The ego is the Achilles heel of man in the warfare between his spirit and flesh. Man's ego is really nothing but a misconceived notion of his self-importance. If the truth is to be told, mankind flesh is of little consequence in the overall scheme of things. He is barely here today and gone tomorrow so to speak. The redeemable entity in mankind is his spirit if such can be duly awakened and transformed into new life in Christ.

Chapter Highlights

- ✓ The exalted realm offers a unique perspective from which to view life on earth in a pure and true light.
- ✓ The willingness to bear the shame and loneliness of the cross is that which validates the truly faithful.
- ✓ To be led in spirit to do the right thing at the right time is to re-build in heavenly order.
- ✓ A confident hope pervades and governs the life of the believer that lives in the kingdom of God.
- ✓ The attributes of Godliness are garnered by the faithful in an unending and everlasting process.
- ✓ There is a divine handwriting in the night sky that most men cannot 'see' due to spiritual blindness.
- ✓ The worthy in faith have been prepared as the nursery for the new age of earth about to unfold.
- ✓ A cosmic silence will happen first before things turn around to point upwards and heavenly.
- ✓ The noble in spirit are woven into the fabric of life to have an inheritance in the good and perfect.
- ✓ The faithful that have been chosen for the new age are bestowed the divine spark that induces life.
- ✓ Man's ego has to be set to naught in order for the spirit of goodness within him to show forth.
- ✓ The ego is the Achilles heel in the warfare between mankind's flesh and the spirit within him.

God's heart is the mansion grand and lovely

The sons are rooms in many hues and colors

Pieces of his heart remade in love and light

As stars of hope to brighten earth's dark veil

Chapter 19

THE SONS WAIT TO SING

The sons of God are being amassed by divine will to be world changers on the grand stage of humanity's affairs. They will be unveiled for all in creation to know and acknowledge only when they reach critical mass. However before the unveiling, the world has to pass through a cleansing that is aimed to sort out things in good order. The world has to pass through a season of disenchantment with illusory grandeur and unbridled consumption so that its taste for the super-sized, glitzy and excessive can subside. It will be like a season of catharsis when a misguided world will be weaned away from the delusion and absurdity of the superfluous. The season of catharsis first has to take place before the unveiling of the sons and the ushering in of the new age of Heaven on earth.

The sons have been spiritually prepared for the works of healing and rebuilding that humanity sorely needs. It is spiritual restoration on a universal scale that evokes the paradise state of Eden. It is restoration of the earth to a new Eden where man, God's favorite creation, can once again walk in fellowship with the heavenly Father. Each son has to know who he has become in Christ before others will come to know him. He has to know before he can learn to use the special services available to him and live up to his true potential. As each son comes to understand the scope of what he can accomplish through the power of God, he must begin the works of restoration for there is little time to waste. Some sons know who they are in Christ but many are yet to fully understand the scope of the power that God has entrusted to them to aid in the healing and restoration of humanity.

The son is that faithful believer who has persevered in faith to grow to full spiritual maturity in Christ. He is the faithful who is communion with the Father and has been availed the gift of the 'comforter'. The 'comforter' is the Holy Ghost and is given so that the recipient can be privy to the heavenly Father's will. He that has received the 'comforter' lives under divine mercy so that he will come to do all things in the spirit of the living God. Such is one who has been measured, found worthy and divinely fitted to be used for works that bring God glory on earth.

The faithful believer who has been fitted for this divine service by God is a vessel calibrated with Christ as the standard of reference. He is able to receive the new wine availed to the faithful through Christ. Such has received a place in God's kingdom as one given to model the way whereby mankind can realize the divine. He will have the right words at the right time for every situation for he is not the one that speaks when he does but the Spirit that dwells within him. In effect, he will become a ruler of men in that whatever he says or does will come to be the order of the day. He is one who no longer strives by his might but given to do the amazing in the Spirit of the living God.

He that has the spirit of life dwelling within to speak through him wields a powerful sword in the service of God. He has to master how to wield the sword through humility and faithful obedience in order to remain victorious over the prince of the darkness of this world. This mastery is crucial as each son embarks on re-creating the earthly in heavenly order. But first the source of the darkness of the world has to be subjugated by divine power acting through the sons before lasting change can come about. Only then can the groundswell to re-create the earth in heavenly order take full effect and lead to the great dawn of humanity. The earth and mankind is God's prized creation but the prince of the darkness of this world has made a mockery of it with his seductive but false ways. He has led humanity away from the way of love down to the path of futility, dissatisfaction, emptiness, diseases, simmering conflicts, hatred, wars and hopelessness. But his time is fast running out as there is an emerging and trending consensus within the hearts of many that there has to be a better way. Deep down in the heart, mankind knows that God did not intend for him to live the way he does and for the earth to be abused the way it is.

The sons of God are bestowed with the mind of Christ so that their will is joined individually and collectively with that of the heavenly Father. The mind of Christ affords the ability to be a good custodian of God's creation. Before his fall, Adam knew what the plants and animals were created for. He understood their purposes and therefore called them by their proper names for his mind was in harmony with that of God. It is that same ability that each son possesses. Each has an innate and instinctive ability to understand what creation and everything within it is designated for. The whole of creation is God's mansion. The sons live in their father's mansion and know what each room and contents are for. They have glimpsed the pattern of things in Heaven and are led by the Spirit of God to 'project' the same on earth. This project of restoration is on-going all over the world as led by the Spirit of God and under a timeline well managed by Divine will.

The sons are called to enlarge their tabernacles so that the seed for the new Heaven on earth can be propagated by their individual and collective actions. By such efforts others will observe their initiatives and subconsciously copy them. It is the will and power of God that acts through those that are called to fulfill diverse divine purposes on earth among mankind. The sons have been predestinated and positioned all over the world in accordance with God's grand plan. No portion of humanity or corner of the earth has been left out so that God will always remain blameless. The sons of light are to be found among all cultures, colors, countries and tongues. The darker the corner of the earth is the purer and more blazing the light within the son positioned there. All the sons embody the universal brotherhood of the living church of Christ and constitute the new Israel.

Each son is connected in spirit to God as an outlet of the divine impetus on earth and as a conduit for those things which flow down from the heavenly throne. In a certain sense the sons can be likened to personal computers that are connected with God the Supercomputer. All due knowledge requisite for the moment is passed on to them from the all-knowing Supercomputer as needed. It is in this context that the Holy Spirit can be likened to the electrical power that energizes the network of computers while the Holy Ghost conveys the information that courses through the network. It is in this way that the sons have cast up the highway to God for their minds are linked up in an information grid through which the wisdom and will of God courses down to earth. But each son must remain sanctified in Truth in order to remain true to that which flows from the throne of God above and reject the false that corrupts borne of the earthy from below.

Truth is the transformer that conditions the power of God to make it effective for doing all kinds of good work. It takes Truth to nullify the attempts of the enemy to stop the spiritual growth and earthly endeavors of the seeker after Christ. Truth prevents and minimizes the damage that the prince of the darkness of this world can inflict on the believer. The believer that has embraced Truth to let it govern his earthly affairs already lives in Godliness. Such a believer who lives his life in the spirit of Truth will always find God to be at hand for him. Truth is also the firewall that shields the knowledge and wisdom entrusted to the faithful from corruption by the enemy. It is the membrane that ideally shields the message of Christ in transmission, conveyance and reception so as to remain pure. It takes Truth to nourish body, mind and spirit in light for it is the essence of the divine and only means to keep evil at bay.

The sons who are connected in spirit to the mind of God are given to understand the mysteries and the sacred hidden truths. They are given access to knowledge precluded from those that deny Truth and the hypocrites that compromise it. It is information communicated to the sons in this light that enables them to be the standard bearers for God that others follow in the light of Christ. And so such live and work to make that which has been conceived in the mind of God to be actualized on earth.

All the sons embody the spirit of regeneration that brings

and sustains new life in the light of Christ. They share and communicate due knowledge within this assembly of renewal through Christ life in truth and love. The assembly is God's mercy program where the chosen are prepared as seedlings for re-creating the earth in new order. Each believer that is part of this assembly may be likened to a nymph that will emerge with God's other sons in due season fitted and entrusted with the knowledge as well as wisdom to 'rule' the earth in heavenly order.

There is always a delay and hesitation before the commitment to answer God's call from when it is first heard. However he who has been divinely earmarked will eventually respond to the call. The response may be gradual because the inertia of worldliness resists change and takes time to be overcome. It takes about three years to build up a commitment to trust God. To let go of the worldly is the spiritual beast that the believer has to wrestle with and overcome before he can stand with Christ. The battle for man's soul is fought between the old life which the believer has known and the new which he is yet to know. Unless God has earmarked him for victory in this fight, the chance for mankind to prevail in this struggle of the old versus new is very slim.

The believer that has won the battle of the old versus the new will thereafter be in the world but no longer belong to it. He will embark on a search guided by the inaudible voice of the Spirit of God to ascertain the Truth as well as power in the words of scripture. Only then has he truly begun to follow in the footsteps of Christ with a good chance of meeting up with him in due time. It takes at least fourteen more years of devoted commitment to mature in the way to meet up with Christ and be ushered into the kingdom of God. There are several ways to aptly describe this spiritual state when the faithful has met up with Christ. It can be said that he has found the room reserved for him in God's mansion or that his soul has become anchored on the solid rock of God. There are numerous other ways of declaring it but the truth is that he has met up with Christ to become reconciled and reconnected with God in spirit.

The believer that has reconnected with God in spirit is much like a lost traveler who has found his way back home by listening for the pulse of Christ. There is a homing device that God has placed in man to serve as a directional finder when needed. This is what it means to be foreknown and pre-destined. But the directional finder can only be powered by Truth and receives only the pulse of Christ. The latter is food to enlighten the soul and revive the dead spirit so the lost can find the way home to God.

Chapter Highlights

- ✓ God has positioned his sons over the world as he works out his plans to give humanity a new start.
- ✓ The sons have been prepared for the healing and restoration of humanity on a universal scale.
- ✓ The faithful that lives by Truth written in his heart will be divinely guided in his endeavors.
- ✓ The faithful fitted for noble service is calibrated with Christ as the standard of reference.
- ✓ The spirit of darkness has to be subjugated through Christ for healing and restoration to take hold.
- ✓ The sons of light have an innate and instinctive understanding of what creation should be like.
- ✓ The sons have been prepositioned by the Divine among all cultures, colors, countries and tongues.
- ✓ Each son of God is a conduit for things which flow from the heavenly throne to reach mankind below.
- ✓ The sons live and work to make that conceived in the mind of God to be actualized on earth.
- ✓ The sons of God are part of the universal web of regeneration that brings and sustains new life.
- ✓ The truly faithful in Christ are guided in spirit to ascertain the Truth and power in God's words.
- ✓ The heart of the faithful believer is linked up with the Divine in love through Truth.

From the starry realm man looks ahead

To the place of good hope and renewal

For backwards leads to a misguided past

To recrimination and accusations galore

Chapter 20

IN THE WILDERNESS

The believer that has fully matured in Christ lives on a spiritual housetop as one given to take the high road in life. It is from there that man's spiritual eye can remain fixed on God as he goes about his calling. He that dwells thereon will be at peace within. He will also have an innumerable company of spiritual messengers at his behest to help him accomplish all that God has assigned for him to do on earth. No one has seen God but the fully matured in Christ are the closest that mankind can come to learn about his nature for they are bestowed with many of his attributes. When mankind begins to seek and call on God sincerely, he will be invariably drawn to one who is matured in spirit to observe and learn from. Any seeker that has one matured in Christ revealed to him must open his heart to receive the gift of enlightenment in love. All who are matured in Christ are God's elect to offer up sacrifices and receive spiritual gifts on behalf of others in love. However such gifts are given freely but there are not free for the faith of the recipient will be sorely tested.

One of the favorite tactics of the enemy of Truth is to put a cloak over the eye of the young believer. He does so by attempting to take him back to the past. The way of Christ offers a new life separate from the past. The two cannot be mixed together but the enemy of God is a master at repackaging the old to look like the new. He cleverly repackages the old in order to beguile and mislead the unwary back to the past that should be left behind. The young believer is a favorite target of the ploys of the enemy aimed at deceiving the young in faith. Quite often the latter are not yet fully established in Christ, may be partaking of God's grace unworthily or struggling to let go of the ungodly ways of the past. A quite effective tactic of the enemy is to falsely accuse the matured in Christ as a blundering heretic with strange ideas so that the young believer may not embrace true light.

The enemy often poses as an angel of light but the Truth is that he works to shield out true light with offerings that turn out to be good for nothing in the end. The enemy is a hypocrite who is never humble or show contrition before God for that is his nature. For that reason, he has been denied the true and fulfilling by God. And so, he works to hinder mankind from receiving same. Humility and true contrition matters a lot with God. The prideful is without contrition in spirit and has unwittingly made room for the enemy in his life. Pride hinders mankind from the fellowship of true light availed through Christ. Fellowship within this elect spiritual company is to be desired by all that seek after Christ for therein true knowledge and divine wisdom abound to be received in love.

The cloak that the prince of darkness attempts to throw over the eye of the believer is usually derived from the traditions and ceremony of the old ways. The old ways becloud the eye of the spirit and impede the intrusion of true light into the heart. It takes total commitment to Christ and a disconnection from the old ways to come into the fellowship of true light. The old has to die before the believer can be transformed in the new light of Christ in divine likeness. The old way funnels mankind into a spiritual coffin but the new way through Christ opens up a new life of endless possibilities.

There should be no room for double mindedness when mankind has chosen the way of Christ. One cannot look backwards and forwards at the same time as he follows after Christ. He will become stagnated in his faith life and not be able to meet up with Christ duly if he does so. This is what many that profess to follow after Christ do when they are beguiled into mixing the old with new. In so doing, they play right into the hands of the enemy. The enemy of true light beguiles the unwary into double-mindedness and uncertainty of faith. First the believer must make the disconnection from the old ways so that he can be able to meet up with Christ. After he has met up with Christ or become spiritually transformed, he will be well prepared to change the old way in the better light of the new. Such is to seek the kingdom of God first before other things and it is the blessed way. Such is wisdom that avails a way of escape from the shackles of the old so that one can afford the new and better in divine light.

The believer that has escaped the old and met up with Christ will be bestowed with the mind of the Master for whom he has left all to seek after. The believer who has met up with Christ has not only grown to full spiritual maturity but has become a son of God as well. He has become prepared in spirit to accomplish such great and marvelous works ordained to bring due God glory. He has become an agent to extend mankind's vision of God so that others can experience divine light and power. God searches very hard to find those worthy of the call of Christ. Many that answer the call prove not to be worthy. Only a few prove to be worthy for many cannot bear the shame and burden of the cross. Those who prove worthy are those that become duly christened as sons of God. There is great joy in Heaven on account of those found worthy of the calling of Christ so that a host of heavenly messengers is at their behest to aid them in all endeavors. With such aid, they are given to go beyond the gates of the known and outside the box of human understanding to where others cannot go. They can go to that place hitherto unknown where a new vista awaits to unfold.

In the Wilderness

The heart that hears and heeds the call of God must be willing to persevere through many challenges. He will be led away by the spirit of the call from all that he has known in the past into a place previously unknown to him. But he must remain committed to Christ so as to be tuned to God and realize the full promises of his new-found land. The spirit of God does not shout as that of the world does. He speaks in a still small voice that is best heard in quiet solitude. And so, the believer is often led away into the wilderness to begin the transformation that leads him to meet up with Christ and into the congregation of the sons. Family, friends and the institutions of his old life will feel let down because he has chosen to put God first in his life above them. But in the fullness of time and with better understanding, many will come to be thankful for the gift of God that he turns out to be for the people.

The faithful in Christ is called not to hold grudges against those that vilify and reject him for many are spiritually ignorant. God saves more of his wrath for those that know but yet sin but less for those that do not know. The faithful that has met up with Christ in the way is asked to deal with all in loving light to share knowledge and wisdom in good faith as needed. He is asked to return to those that lack such to share Truth and wisdom in the light of Christ. It takes such light to highlight the way into the new place where the earthly meets the heavenly. He that has matured in the light of Christ knows that with the passage of time many will come to understand God's way better. They will come to realize that God chooses sons in order to offer them as living sacrifices acceptable for the sins of the people and that many are appointed to embrace Truth through them to find new life. It is by the willingness to suffer on behalf of others that the sons of God demonstrate the nature of divine love.

In the quest to meet up with the divine, many that seek for spiritual fulfillment in the light of Christ do so in the wrong places. They seek in different temples and various places of worship but often fail to find fulfillment thereabouts. This is usually the case when the believer begins to mature in spirit for only the true will fulfill him then. With spiritual maturity, some do come to realize that God is not to be found in a temple of mortar and bricks. Spiritual communion with the Divine does not take place in buildings or groups but in time spent alone seeking to know God better. The time spent in the churches of bricks and mortar serves an introduction to the truth and reality of God. However Christ or the connection to God can only be made by each seeker alone through the heart.

There is a time in spiritual growth when the truly faithful will be called in spirit to venture out into the lonely wilderness so that he can meet up with Christ and thereby come to know the heavenly Father. The true congregation of God is the church without walls and it is found in the lonely wilderness of life by the true seeker. It is much like a mountain located away from the known and familiar that the faithful are called to climb. Often as true seekers are called away from their midst, the churches with walls devolve into congregations of the worldly in spirit where the lust after earthly material assumes primary focus.

And so to mask this truth, the churches with walls often adopt a false posture which equates appearance and material acquisitions as proof of spiritual worthiness before God. But nothing can be further from the truth. The churches with walls or buildings in which people meet in his name do not constitute God's temple. The true temple is the man whose heart God has chosen to be his point of contact with humanity. He is the man whose heart has been washed and whose soul has been purified by Truth. The heart of such a man is the altar of God lit by the flame of love. The man whose heart has been chosen in this light has come into God's confidence. He will be informed of God's will as necessary for he has been led into the commonwealth of the living church of Christ. This congregation embodies the spirits of the justified before God through Christ. The 'heart of God' is the aggregate of such hearts that have been chosen by God as his temple. It is the hub of regeneration where the old becomes new and the dead spring back to new life through Christ.

In the Wilderness

Each man whose heart is chosen as a temple of the Divine is availed knowledge about significant events to come as due for God will not do anything without letting them know. God is spiritually connected to such that are his temples so that he wills and acts through them as sons to accomplish his divine purposes on earth. To be used in this light is a calling and a way of life ordained for the sons from the foundation of time. It is for this that they were called away from their past lives to be remade in the image of Christ. All remade in that wise must return to offer the new way to their own from whose midst they were called away. Sadly the sons are often not embraced as should but rather rejected. However such rejection never stymies the sons for they will draw others who are 'strangers' to them. Every son that his own rejects will be embraced by others who were not formerly of his own kind for Truth never returns void. In truth God will make sons from any erstwhile sinner willing to embrace light.

Every son is an elect person of destiny who will be known from birth to be a chosen one. All the circumstances and experiences of his life will aggregate to fit the profile of Christ in accordance with the template defined by the words of scriptures. These include questions about his birth circumstances, parentage, heritage, education, struggles, rejection and rebirth in new spirit. Regardless of the tribe, tongue and color the profile is the same. Every son is usually born in the seemingly nondescript house.

In the Wilderness

This is usually the 'little' house, in the 'little' village but yet he will be of an illustrious linage that can be traced back to the distant past. There is always a sign from the sky when such a one comes into this world and when they depart. Even as children, the elect sons are known to be destined for special missions on earth. However they are often misunderstood while their mission is on-going until the season appointed for it to be understood.

The special mission is a 'new' strange way that had not been known or anticipated by the people. Time always shows the new way to be spiritually uplifting, enlightening, fulfilling and far better than what had been known before. The new is the way of peace and compassion where there is no need for strife. The new way removes the shackles and bondage of the old way so that the willing can be set free to grow in true light to commune with God. The elect sons are universal sprits who travel as emissaries from heavenly to lowly places. They are sent to uplift mankind in spirit so as to realize a better vision of God. They return at the completion of their earthly duties to the heavenly home from whence they are sent down.

Each elect son can be likened to a step in a divine escalator or cosmic wheel that turns from Heaven down to earth and upwards again to rejoin the divine realm. Whoever embraces the way of the elect will be lifted up along with them into the heavenly heights from whence each came down originally. Each elect son has the innate ability to overcome the hold of the world because the inner man of his spirit is conditioned by love of Truth to buoyantly list heavenwards away from the earthen. The sons are the light of the world given as God's gifts to help chase out darkness from humanity's midst. They are used to model the way for those who desire to know God better. Each son is called to share wisdom with those that lack as reasonable service to God and as the means to help them find answers to life's problems in love through light. It is for this reason that they are always and attack by the prince of darkness who seeks to halt the spread of Truth and light. But the sons carry on because they know that the sooner that many embrace Truth is the sooner that the hold of the prince of darkness on the world will be loosed.

Each son of God is a ground breaker called to be a rebuilder of the broken down and a builder of the new in light and love. For this reason he will be under the attack of the prince of darkness. But the attacks of the enemy never deter such that have grown in grace to stand before God under mercy. The attacks do not deter the truly faithful because God is their shield and protection from the enemy. In a paradoxical way, every attack withstood leads to a place closer to the heart of God and to a greater outpouring of divine anointing on the faithful.

Chapter Highlights

- ✓ The matured in spirit dwells on a 'housetop' where his spiritual eyes are always fixed on God.
- ✓ God's gifts are given freely but there are not free for the faith of the receiver will always be tested.
- ✓ The believer must disconnect from the old ways to realize spiritual maturity and divine fellowship.
- ✓ The enemy of God beguiles the unwary by getting mankind to look backwards instead of forwards.
- ✓ God speaks in a still small voice best heard in the quiet solitude of suffering and world's rejection.
- ✓ God is displeased with those that know but do not and less with those who know not and so do not.
- ✓ God's temple is not of bricks and mortars but the heart chosen to be his point of contact on earth.
- ✓ The prism of the old ways distorts the light of God but the lens of the new framed in Christ focuses it.
- ✓ The life circumstances and experiences of every son of God will mirror the profile of Christ.
- ✓ Every attack of the enemy that the believer withstands leads closer to the heart of God.
- ✓ The cross that the faithful endure in compassion with Christ is the bridge into the eternal realm.
- ✓ The sons may suffer in the world but God's doting love proves more than enough to heal their pain.

The man that strives for noble service

Is given to live in immunity of godliness

For the past has been made impotent

And powerless to harm his golden soul

Chapter 21

FROM THE SACRIFICE OF ONE

The matured in Christ being those that have met up to be bonded in spirit with him through faith are the vicars appointed by God through whom divine grace reaches young believers in love. They are like faucets out of which God's living water flows to reach those that thirst for it. The flow of grace is of utmost importance in maintaining the nursery of young believers in the way of Christ. Grace covers the young believer during his most vulnerable years when the enemy is hard at work trying to extinguish his flickering faith. It is harder for the enemy to lead astray those believers who have established some foothold in the way of Christ than with the young.

Just as the parents or older siblings provide help in love for young ones in a family, so also does grace operate through the more established in faith to provide protection and stability for the less established in Christ. Grace flows like milk through the nipple that the elder offers up so that the younger can afford vital spiritual food to nourish him in light and love. It is nourishment that affords spiritual strength to uphold the young believer when he does not yet have strong spiritual legs to stand on. And so grace works through the light and love of Christ to provide a safety net in the formative years of faith. The young believer who remains faithful in light will eventually grow from leaning on grace to stand before God in mercy.

It is by faithful obedience to Truth that believers are able to mature spiritually in the light of Christ to stand before God under mercy and the young can continue to grow in faith. Those that are matured in spirit are called to provide coverage to the young in faith in much the same way as their predecessors provided for them. The young believer can have this coverage from his elders in faith by grace when he faithfully follows after them in light after the footsteps of Christ. Grace is the medium by which the essence of Christ is shared to lead the faithful on to mercy. It is about sharing gifts with others in love in a way that helps the spread of light and growth of the kingdom of God. However, for the unfaithful that is after gain, the window of grace often comes to an unexpected end when he least expects it. Such is often the lot of the false confessor whose heart idolizes the things of the world rather than the heavenly.

Grace is based on the spiritual tenet that when the bridegroom is there, the children of the bride chamber do not fast. The spiritually matured in Christ is the vicar shepherd as well as the bridegroom in this light whereas the children are the young believers who are charged to him in grace. The vicar shepherd willingly bears the burden of the spiritually young. In the old way of Moses, everyone is accountable for themselves in matters of faith after a certain age. Beyond that age, all are deemed to know right from wrong. In that tradition, physical age as well as religious and political correctness count for much in that those attributes are oftentimes equated with knowledge and wisdom. It is not so in the new way of Christ. Physical age, worldly knowledge or external appearance is not an indicator of faithfulness in the way of Christ. Strong faith comes with maturity of spirit within the believer and is less about physical age or outside appearance.

And so, the faithful believer who is young in age may be spiritually alive through Christ whereas an older person in age may be spiritually dead. In the new way of Christ, which is about sharing, he that is spiritually strong is called to hold up the one that is spiritually weak until such a time as the weaker is rooted and established in faith. Christ calls the elder to wash the feet of the spiritually young. It is incumbent on the elder to wash the dirt of transgression off the feet of the young until God commands otherwise for the things concerning Christ do come to an end. There is always an appointed season when the window of grace closes so the door of mercy can open for the faithful.

For the follower after Christ, baptism in spirit precedes the close of the window of grace. Spiritual baptism is the demarcation point between grace and mercy. It is the milestone that separates the earth-stuck from the heaven-bound. Beyond that point, the truly faithful will be duly acknowledged by the heavenly Father as a son in accordance with divine will. He that is so acknowledged has grown to connect spiritually with the three dimensions of the triune God to live under divine mercy. He is one that has met up with Christ to become a good shepherd of the flock in love. The good shepherd lives for the flock for he is the medium through whom grace reaches them. The young in faith are mostly oblivious of the reach of the flow of the grace from the Divine through the shepherd to the flock. In their spiritual ignorance, the young in faith are often presumptuous and not really appreciative of the fact that the vicar shepherd is used to divinely avail much to them in grace. Since they only know in part, the young often take grace for granted and are not very well informed about its vicarious nature and implications.

Often the young believer lives in violation of the laws of God but do not suffer the consequences because he is under the charge of a vicar that suffers on his behalf in love. The vicar shepherd sacrifices much so that the young believer can be shielded and provided for in light and love. Every good shepherd is given to make sacrifices as needed in love through Christ so that goodness can abound among humanity. They sacrifice in the hope that in due season the young who has been covered by grace will mature in spirit to stand on own faith. The faithful believer that has grown in faith to stand under divine mercy is in turn expected to provide spiritual coverage through grace to those that follow after him in Christ. As he was once charged to another, others will now come under his spiritual charge. Unless one has come into true knowledge of God, he cannot lay down his life to shepherd others in love and have them live vicariously through him.

The close of the window of grace has to take place before the door of mercy can open for the faithful to meet up with Christ. God determines the season of the close of the window of grace and not the believer. However as the end of grace approaches, both the Holy Spirit and the Holy Ghost will begin to feature significantly in the believer's life. This is a time of upward spiritual transition when the believer who has faithfully embraced Truth under the love and charge of a vicar shepherd will spiritually grow to be established in the light of Christ. The believer that has been well nurtured in Christ by his vicar will be connected in spirit with him so that the latter will always be in him. Even as he matures to stand on his own faith, the power of God will still flow through the vicar to reach his charge. It is in this way that Christ comes to live in spiritual sons through their fathers within a commonwealth of those that are faithful in light.

The years of the season of grace are fraught with the danger of presumption and feeling of entitlement for the young believer. He may come to feel that the laws of God may be violated with little or no consequences. Furthermore, he may come to be quite dismissive and neglectful of those that nurture and cover him in grace. It is for this reason that many who are young in faith lose their way and are not able to grow into spiritual maturity in Christ as due. They become stagnant in their faith walk to end up in an arrested spiritual development. Many wither away spiritually on account of willfulness and refusal to fully embrace the mentoring shepherd ordained for them. Such may look like faithful followers on the outside but lack the spiritual roots within to enable them stand upright in the light of Christ.

Sadly, many young believers are not able to receive the full benefits of the vicar divinely appointed for them. In refusing to fully embrace Truth, they neglect to exercise the use of the 'right hand' which soon withers away. The right hand symbolizes the hand of faith and fortuity that is needed to receive the good and perfect gifts divinely appointed for man to have. All gifts that are fulfilling, sustainable and enduring issue forth from heavenly places and are received with the right hand of faith. In being dismissive of the vicar, those that are unfaithful to Truth fail to grow in spirit and to avail themselves of the blessings of faith through Christ. Such that are unfaithful to Truth preclude the goodness and mercy of God from reaching them because they lack the hand to receive.

There is a time of separation and a sorting out process by which the child of grace becomes the man of God able to stand under mercy. This sorting out process marks the transition when the faithful is called to put his spiritual house in order. This is when the template for victorious living is written into the hearts of those appointed to meet up with Christ. Baptism in the water of truth spawns many disciples but only a few out of the lot will continue in faithfulness to meet up with Christ. Many hearts will be washed with God's truth but only a few will be baptized in the fire of the spirit of Christ. The transition from grace to mercy is when the vine that has produced good fruit is pruned so as to produce even more and the unfruitful vine is cut down. It is a time when the bridegroom is taken away so that the children of the bride chamber can begin to fast. The sorting out process closes the window of grace but opens the door of goodness and mercy for it signals the transition of the child to the 'man of God'.

The realm of goodness and mercy is where the faithful receives his 'new name' in God. It ushers in a shifting away from the old way to a new way of doing things. This new way is separate and distinct from the old. The flock of God thins out for there is no child to be found therein but men. Therein is where allowance is no longer made for violation of the kingdom of God. All who partake of and violate grace unworthily do not make it into the realm of mercy. They that violate grace on account of love of the worldly cannot afford the heavenly. Such are they that are unwilling to make necessary sacrifices but choose rather to love God with conditions and within limits.

Adequate time has been divinely appointed so that every tree can be established to produce fruit. Many have produced bad fruits but an adequate number have produced good fruits. Those who partook of grace worthily through Christ have produced good fruits. Such no longer live selfishly for themselves but share as they receive in a spirit of universal brotherhood. They do not withhold any gift but rather encourage and hope for others to receive those things which they themselves have received. Those who have proven to be fruitful in this wise do continue as new branches of Christ in the kingdom of God. Such are the worthy given to bear many sons in like image for God. The vicar shepherd embodies the love that willingly sacrifices all for the welfare of the beloved flock. He is often under-appreciated by many but he is much beloved by the heavenly Father for nobility of heart and purity of purpose. Faithfulness in light is vicarious living and he that seeks after Godliness must learn to live for others.

Chapter Highlights

- ✓ Grace flows through the saintly in spirit to sustain the nursery of young believers in love.
- ✓ Grace is the safety net that upholds the believer and protects him from the wiles of the enemy.
- ✓ The transition from grace on to mercy is the divine dynamic that determines spiritual maturity.
- ✓ Physical age and worldly knowledge is not an indicator of faith but maturity of the spirit within is.
- ✓ It is incumbent in the kingdom way to wash the dirt of transgression off the feet of the young in faith.
- ✓ There is a demarcation point separating grace from mercy beyond which the heavenly is manifested.
- ✓ Only the fully matured in spirit can live the life that sacrifices all on account of love for others.
- ✓ Grace is often accompanied by presumption and a feeling of entitlement by the spiritually blind.
- ✓ The right hand embodies faith and fortuity needed to receive the good gifts appointed on to man.
- ✓ There is a time of separation when the child of grace becomes the man able to stand under mercy.
- ✓ The realm of mercy is where neither child nor violator is found but only true men of God.
- ✓ The faithful withhold not those gifts received but rather share in loving hope with others in the way.

A divine light is evoked by true confession

As the heart finds agreement with the tongue

Such a great release and freedom from guilt

With peace and serenity as welcome suitors

Chapter 22

SCRIPT FOR A NEW LIFE

The divine way calls on those who have more to share in love with those that have less and the stronger in faith to make accommodation for the weaker in Christ. The way of light is about sharing so that by the sacrifices of one many others may come to be uplifted. The 'christened' in light comes to minister to others and not to be ministered to. The master serves the servant so that both can become better for it. He washes the feet of the servant so that the transgressor can be led on to the righteous path. Such is the unfathomable way of God and the efficacy of grace that one part within the body can make the whole better. He that has laid down his life for the welfare of the flock is the true shepherd given to pick it up again in due season in greater glory. The due season is a time of regeneration when new life springs forth out of the carcass of the old.

Regeneration comes about when the believer has sought and found the way into the kingdom of God. It can never be realized unless the profession of the mouth is the true confession of the heart. Truth has found a welcome home in the believer when the confession of his heart is in harmony with the profession of his mouth. Truth has come alive in the believer when he walks in the light always so that his words and actions differ not. When this becomes the case, there is a sense of release and freedom of purpose that governs the spirit. Inevitably, a sense of peace and serenity also follow suit.

To embrace Truth brings the believer into a place of sharper focus and purpose where great vision is availed. The believer that seeks new life through Christ will always be guided by the spirit of Truth through Bethany. He that is spiritually guided to Bethany has learned to tarry for the Divine to lead in all earthly endeavors. There in Bethany is where the old self dies in the way in seeking after Christ so that a new self can rise from the carcass. Bethany is the place of ascension where the newly reborn in the spirit of Christ rises up for rendezvous with the divine Father. It is where the tears of the believer are wiped away. Death is the most grievous event that can befall man but there in Bethany is where the spirit is freed to rise to the exalted heights where death cannot touch it. If victory over death can be found in Bethany so also can the answers to all of life's problems. Bethany is the blank sheet given to the man of strong faith and great vision to write a new script for his life. It is the virgin plot of land that the faithful can cultivate with seeds of righteousness.

True confession yields great power for mankind in that it harmonizes the flesh with the spirit. True confession is the medium by which the two old enemies of the spirit and flesh find concord. When this is achieved within the heart of the faithful, the hidden truths of the scriptures will become revealed to him. The true confessor will begin to eat meat with Christ. All that God will ever communicate to man has already been done and woven into the words of scripture. Albeit man can only know as he is known. Wherever true confession exists so that the flesh and spirit are in concord is where peace that passes understanding comes to make a home. The believer that has found such peace will be able to search out all hidden matters. Nothing can remain hidden for long to him that is given to search out the veiled truths.

The heart without blemish and justified before God will know the needful things for he is a mirror polished by God's perfecting hand. The heart that is so polished will possess a mind that will reflect the Divine. The heavenly Father will not conceal anything from such a heart for he has earned divine trust. Such is a heart that serves the divine will with the perseverance of Job and cries to God with the deeply painful remorse of David. The mind with such a heart will be uplifted to intermeddle with divine wisdom. To intermeddle with wisdom in this light is to be bestowed with the key of knowledge so that all things will be duly revealed as due and needed.

True confession is the seed of faith and costs nothing but the sacrifice of the ego. It is the process by which the flesh begins to yield to the spirit and the primer for the dynamic that does the work of the kingdom of God. The dynamic is twofold and comprises the Holy Ghost as well as the Holy Spirit. The Holy Ghost communicates to the mind of man as the medium by which he logs in to the divine mind. The Holy Spirit motivates the life force and enables the body. It is the medium by which man connects to divine power.

Both the Holy Ghost and Holy Spirit are necessary for accomplishing the glorious works of the kingdom of God. Without the Holy Ghost the believer is led into action by his own will and not God's whereas without the Holy Spirit he runs in his own strength. He that runs in his own strength will inevitably weary as he runs, faint as he walks and not be uplifted in spirit to connect with the Divine. He that labors without the Holy Ghost and the Holy Spirit will not be under the mercy of God. He will not have a good reward for his efforts for he will labor outside of divine will. It takes the Holy Ghost to keep the believer well informed for only then can he afford the patience to tarry for God plans to be worked out for him. By the same token, the Holy Spirit comes to bear in the life of the believer when it is time to no longer tarry but act.

Without the Holy Ghost, the believer is like one that stumbles around in darkness. He may have the willingness and the energy but he will lack true vision and proper guidance to accomplish his goal. He is liable to follow the rush of the human horde and go along with the blind. He will become like one that shoots in a dark alley who hopes to hit some target out there. But without the Holy Spirit, the believer is like one that attempts to roll the proverbial boulder up the hill but without success. He will fall short every time for the task will always be more than he can handle. He will not be able to get over the hump. The impossible becomes possible with both the Holy Ghost and Holy Spirit engaged in mankind's endeavors.

Earthly endeavors become pointless in the end without the Holy Ghost and fruitless without the Holy Spirit. The Holy Ghost when combined with the Holy Spirit will work together to overcome all things to serve God's divine purposes. The believer who tarries to be informed by the Holy Ghost before acting is 'Mary'. She represents the believer who holds out for the mind of Christ. The believer who seeks to plug in to the power of the Holy Spirit is 'Martha'. The believer who is neither plugged in nor logged on is 'Lazarus' dead in the tomb. But the believer who is both logged on to the information of the Holy Ghost and plugged into the power of the Holy Spirit is Lazarus arisen from the sleep of death.

Lazarus arisen is the manifestation of life over death that is sought after by the faithful. It is the subservience of the earthen to the Divine. The faithful has to love Christ before he can come into Bethany. The faithful believer has to spiritually grow into Bethany so that he can find resurrection of spirit and new life as Lazarus did. He that has found new life in Christ must take the napkin off his mouth and begin to declare about the reality and the goodness of God as the Holy Ghost informs him. He must yield so that the burial bandages can be taken off from his hands. When his hands are free is when he will be able to serve in good faith as the Holy Ghost informs him. He must yield so that the burial bandages can be taken off from his feet. It is only when his feet are free that he can follow as the Holy Spirit leads. It is only when the believer has been freed from the trappings of his past life that can he step into the new life to eat meat with Christ and be covered in the fragrance of the good work acceptable to God.

Chapter Highlights

- ✓ It is by the efficacy of grace that one part within the body can make the whole lot better.
- ✓ There is a sense of release and freedom of spirit that governs the heart when man speaks in truth.
- ✓ The faithful that has found new life through Christ can find answers to life's myriad problems.
- ✓ True confession is the medium by which the old enemies of the spirit and flesh find concord.
- ✓ The faithful that is justified before God is a mirror polished by the Divine to be without blemish.
- ✓ True confession is the seed of faith that costs nothing except the sacrifice of the ego.
- ✓ The impossible becomes possible where both the Holy Ghost and Holy Spirit are engaged with man.
- ✓ Spiritual rebirth is the manifestation of life over death sought by believers and availed by Christ.

The Spirit finds freedom by ascension

To the exalted realm of glory above

Where life abounds freed from death

There to dine amidst Divine company

Books for Spiritual Guidance by Kalu Onwuka

Nuggets of Resurrection is an engaging discourse that explores the many gifts available to the spiritually matured in Christ, the path that seekers are called to walk as well as how to overcome challenges along the way.

Pulses of the Divine Heart is an uplifting and enriching study that attests to the abiding nature of God's love and the unfailing goodness of Providence to the faithful man whose spirit is in tune with the divine.

Etching for the Heart is a timely, fascinating and insightful study that highlights the power of sacrificial love, good hope and the enlightenment of Christ to bring wholeness in life of the believer.

No Hurry to Horeb is a thoughtful discourse about how mankind can tune his inner awareness to rise above the lowliness of today's society and realize the fullness of life divinely appointed for those who truly aspire.

Echoes of the Golden thoughtfully and deeply explores the path that leads to spiritual transformation so that mankind can begin to see from a heavenly perspective to make the earthly experience better.

Books of Original Poems by Kalu Onwuka

Anthems in the Glorious Dawn is a rich collection of ninety-three original poems to nourish the soul, uplift the spirit and help rekindle a relationship with God. The underlying message of the power of sacrificial love strikes a resonant chord.

In Enchantment of Eternity is a superb collection of ninety-four original poems that touches the heart deeply through such topics as love, the treasures of life's high road as well as the vision and victory availed through strong faith.

Tones of the Stellar is a volume of eighty eight inspirational poems that speaks to the freedom of spirit and wholeness of life availed by enlightenment through Christ. The remarkable verses offer guidance about reconnecting with God.

A Splendid Awakening is a simple yet eloquent collection of ninety-two inspirational poems that highlights how man must let go of his mistake-laden past to realize a fulfilling and enduring future full of God's blessing.

 *The Melody of Light* is a selection from the author's body of work that represents the very best of faith-based poetry. Brimming with insights and thoughtful lessons, the verses paint vivid images about the wholeness that love avails.

All titles are available as paperbacks or e-books and may be purchased through many retail outlets and on-line distribution channels including **amazon.com**. All titles may also be purchased through Granada Publishers at **www.granadapublishing.com** and excerpts of the author's work are available at **www.kaluonwuka.com**.

Kalu Onwuka is a prolific author who writes about faith-walk and the path to transformation within for better in this new age of spiritual awareness. A vanguard among the emerging breed of spiritual poets, he uses his works to highlight the path that mankind must walk in order to find a blissful balance between the earthly and the heavenly.

He is the author of *Ruminations on the Golden Strand* series which are in-depth studies based on spiritual and earthly experiences that frame modern living in a way to help mankind achieve the utmost within a relationship with the Divine. The series include *Nuggets of Resurrection, Pulses of the Divine Heart, Etching for the Faithful Heart, No Hurry to Horeb,* and *Echoes of the Golden.*

He is also the author of *Poems in Faithfulness to the Divine* series which are books of poetry and songs. These include *Anthems in the Glorious Dawn, In Enchantment of Eternity, Tones of the Stellar, A Splendid Awakening* and *The Melody of Light.* There are other works on the way including the forthcoming *Capsules of Divine Splendor.*

Onwuka is a teacher, poet, lyricist, electrical engineer and entrepreneur. He lives in California with his wife of many years with whom he has raised five children. As a follower of Christ Jesus as the Light of the world, he believes that all true spiritual paths eventually converge in Christ. He uses his writing to help many achieve spiritual transformation for a more fulfilling life.

www.ingramcontent.com/pod-product-compliance
Lightning Source LLC
Chambersburg PA
CBHW060150050426
42446CB00013B/2762